• A HISTORY LOVER'S •
GUIDE TO
AUSTIN

• A HISTORY LOVER'S •
GUIDE TO
AUSTIN

JASON WEEMS

Foreword by Harrison Eppright

THE
History
PRESS

Published by The History Press
Charleston, SC
www.historypress.com

Front cover, clockwise from top left: Statue of Eeyore the Donkey at Eastwoods Park; Austin skyline seen through colored glass in the Austin Central Library; The Goddess of Liberty crowns the Texas State Capitol Building dome; *Rhapsody* mosaic by Professor John Yancey at Dr. Charles Urdy Plaza.
Back cover, top: Completed maypole at Eeyore's Birthday Party at Pease Park; *bottom*: Littlefield Fountain and UT Tower at University of Texas–Austin.
All photos and illustrations by the author unless otherwise noted.

First published 2021

ISBN 9781540246424

Library of Congress Control Number: 2020948767

Notice: The information in this book is true and complete to the best of our knowledge. It is offered without guarantee on the part of the author or The History Press. The author and The History Press disclaim all liability in connection with the use of this book.

This book is dedicated…
To my friends and family for a lifetime of love and support.
To Austinites for the home and community you've given me.
To Austin, may you ever be a sanctuary for the dreamers and a
monument to their dreams.

CONTENTS

CONTENTS

CONTENTS

FOREWORD

A ustin is one of the fastest-growing cities in the United States and among the top cities to visit and recommend for return visits. The natural beauty, geography, hospitality, attitudes and history have beckoned visitors and potential residents for over fifteen thousand years. A quote from Mr. Weems's book is apt: "The same breathtaking beauty that draws more than fifty-five thousand new residents to Austin each year has drawn human life to the comfortable climes for longer than we can truly comprehend."

Jason is, like me, a tour guide, historian, one who is passionate about Austin's rich history, natural beauty and its creativity. Austin is known as the Live Music Capital of the World. Speaking of creativity, in addition to being an outstanding tour guide and historian, Jason is also a singer-songwriter, a contributor to Austin's aforementioned live music moniker, so Jason is uniquely qualified to write a guide to Austin.

Jason's book shares with you the stories of some of Austin's legendary figures, household names such as the city's namesake Stephen F. Austin, Sam Houston, Lyndon Baines Johnson and Lady Bird Johnson, but also Angelina Eberly, Azie Taylor Morton, Clara Driscoll, Isamu Taniguchi and Emma S. Barrientos.

Come and explore the legend of lost gold along Shoal Creek, which interested an ambitious young man within the employ of the Texas Land Office, who would later make a name for himself in the literary world. Also check out the story of the woman who fired the "shot heard 'round Austin," ensuring that Austin would remain the capital of the young Republic of

Texas. And don't forget the story of "Custer's Field," named for an area where the Seventh Cavalry once camped and was commandeered by *that* General Custer.

Jason shows you how Austinites—as Austin residents are called—have continuously claimed and reclaimed spaces and landmarks, including a bridge in downtown Austin that is home to the largest urban bat colony in North America, for the enjoyment of visitors and residents alike. Learn how all this (and more) makes up the natural, cultural and creative DNA of Austin, and see for yourself why Austin has become such a unique city.

Welcome to Austin—the capital of Texas, the City of the Violet Crown, the Live Music Capital of Texas, the Friendly City. And remember to "Keep Austin Weird"!

—HARRISON DAVID EPPRIGHT
Manager of Visitor Services and Tour Ambassador at Visit Austin
Tour Docent for SixSquare: Austin's Black Cultural District
Tour Docent at the Driskill Hotel
Host of *Juneteenth Jamboree* on KLRU/PBS

AUTHOR'S NOTE

I cannot tell a lie."

That famous line is, of course, attributed to a young George Washington. From the earliest possible age, I knew, despite popular misconception, that the cherry tree tale was a fiction created to give historical substance to a fledgling young nation. This awareness wasn't due to some great understanding on my part as a child but rather because the author of that story, along with many other stories of our nation's founding fathers, was a hero in my childhood home. You see, the man behind the myths, Parson Mason Locke Weems, was one of my ancestors and arguably the forefather my family is the proudest of. Countless were the times in my childhood when I was told of his stint as Washington's pastor before the war and his life as a traveling author, musician and orator when the Revolution was through.

It seems obvious, in hindsight, that I might seek to emulate in my own lifestyle a path not so different from this ancestral hero. I reached adulthood and took up a career as a Texas troubadour, which is to say I've lived my life as a touring singer-songwriter, master of ceremonies and collector and sharer of stories. The skills honed over a lifetime as a performer and event producer are actually quite similar to those required of a tour guide, and after a long summer of musical touring and festival production in 2014, I decided to put down some roots back home in Austin. I took a job as the first guide with a then fledgling company called Austin Detours offering experiences that, when not paused by a global pandemic, have become the most purchased tourist tickets sold in the state of Texas.

After spending some time with my guests at Austin Detours, I quickly came to realize that my mission, at its heart, should be to help people personally connect to the stories of our city, and to accomplish that I must undo the work of people like my old hero, Parson Weems. If I really want to bring these stories to life, then I need to be able to show that these were real people who were more than mere names to be recited and that these times were not so very long ago. For the stories to become personal, one must be able to see that though the circumstances may have been extreme, it was a human, just like you and me but faced with impossible choices, at the heart of every amazing yarn or tale of revolution. The men and women who came before us deserve to have their humanity preserved, and that includes their struggles, their foibles and their charms. To de-mythologize the times, events and people of our history is to return the legacy of those men and women into the hands of the ordinary, everyday folks who have yet to learn that a hero or a legend may just lie dormant inside of them, too. Perhaps with this perspective we will all be inspired to be more participatory in the choices we make and do more than just watch history unfold continually before our eyes.

That constant unfolding of history brings us to some informative points about my approach to writing this book and the subjects that I selected. First, the obvious point should be stated that history is infinite in its facets, and providing a complete retelling is simply impossible. In this book I've tried to spotlight certain locations that are relevant to our story based on their own merits, and I've organized them in geographical order focusing on just five areas of town, which, I admit, is to omit many other relevant places and stories. This was a wrenching process, and I made the choices presented in this book based on a variety of criteria.

A person could read this work as a collection of short stories about Austin, or you can take it out on a physical outing around the town and use it to enhance your exploration. You'll find that the next location you'll read about is almost always right around the corner from where the last subject left off. When these vignettes are placed in context to each other, it is my hope that the reader will see a larger tale of Austin emerge. I've personally found a great deal of inspiration in the history of this place and these people. I'm fascinated that this city was purpose built and that our citizens have always pushed the boundaries of culture, music, art, science and technology. I find it interesting that Austin has developed such a distinct and influential culture and that our population has grown at breakneck speed as the world clamors to be a part of this modern moment.

The collective exuberance for all things Austin speaks volumes about what and who has come before, and it's my hope that the reader will leave this book more equipped to recognize the true roots of this thriving age among the stories and structures it was all built upon.

The perceptive reader might notice an absence of local bars, restaurants or music venues in these pages. All of these beloved businesses being so central to who we are, any objection to the omission is valid. The year 2020, in which this book was written, has been an infamous experience to live through and especially impactful for Austin due to the necessary closing of the tourism industry. One of the things a global pandemic will do to a town like Austin, a town whose heart is in its meeting spots, is show how vulnerable restaurants and bars can be to collectively falling off an unexpected economic cliff. As a direct result of the prolonged shutdowns that we've faced in Austin this year, many of our most beloved gathering places, like in so many other towns, have been forced by circumstances to shutter. Sadly, many of those closures will likely become permanent. Watching this massive loss of cultural resources occur in real time around me while writing this book was striking and likely influenced my decision to focus on more permanent public places of note, leaving the detailed recommendations of where to eat and what shows to catch to your tour guides or local contacts instead.

On a more philosophical note, I feel it's important to add that history is often morally complicated and messy, and especially so when looking back at a very different time with the perspective of our modern paradigms. It's important that we have the courage to review our most troubling episodes with open eyes and let the stories speak for themselves. We should acknowledge when our traditional heroes are flawed, and we should strive to see those shortcomings in the context of their times. All of this is to say that we must not shy away from uncomfortable subjects such as racism. To do so would be to tell an incomplete story of Austin, while turning our backs on our most inspirational figures who thrived despite the obstacles and blazed their own trails for themselves and for all of us, regardless of race or station, who've come behind them. By learning the humanity of these tales, we discover our heroes and diminish our villains, and that allows us to take something of worth away from that moment spent interrogating our past.

The struggles of all of those who have come before us can inform us. To say the history of Austin belongs to this man or that, to this group or that, is simply false and limiting. The history of our town is one of invention, and of poets, and of dreamers. It's a story of fate made manifest and of bravery, blood and sacrifice. It's also the story of oppression and emancipation. It's a story of race relations and of the people who fought to overcome oppressive systems, along with the occasional mention of those who fought to preserve those systems. In Austin's journey, we continue to evolve as a people. That evolution, for the most part, has been one that has progressed (sometimes slowly) toward inclusion and acceptance for all of our citizens, and this progressive persona is central to the identity we collectively present to the world today.

This book is but a sliver of the history of our people, and all of us have been shaped in one way or another by these tales even if we aren't aware of their constant influence. In the end, it's how we treat one another that history recalls the most vividly. In this modern age, we see renewed interests from all sides about these deeply moving topics of interrelation, and it shows that these topics are still the things that shape us the most. When approaching these tender subjects in this book, I often chose to focus on the figures I've come across and the stories I've learned that have been an inspiration to me personally or that were obviously significant to our larger story. I came to see a pattern when researching, where I found that the most interesting stories often lay somewhere between the period of a definitive statement and the first capital letter of the next sentence in the official accounts or reference materials. The more I could dig between the lines, the more humanity I would find, and those are the stories that most often made it onto these pages.

It has been an immense pleasure and a true honor to craft this book for you, dear reader. I hope you find as much inspiration for your own adventures by reading its pages as I've found in researching and writing them. Whether you're exploring Austin in spirit or in person, as a local or as a guest, get out there and enjoy the town. And don't just watch history unfold; make a little history too and give me something to write about!

With gratitude,
Jason Weems

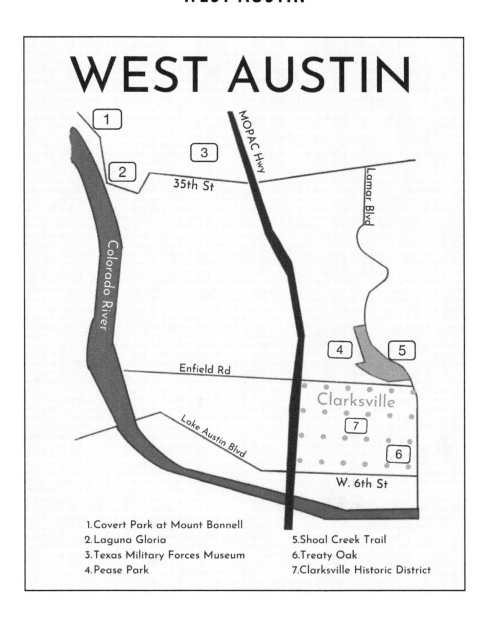

WEST AUSTIN

1. Covert Park at Mount Bonnell
2. Laguna Gloria
3. Texas Military Forces Museum
4. Pease Park
5. Shoal Creek Trail
6. Treaty Oak
7. Clarksville Historic District

COVERT PARK AT MOUNT BONNELL

3800 Mount Bonnell Road

There are few better places to begin an exploration of Austin, Texas, than Mount Bonnell. The unparalleled view of the city offered here will help you get the lay of the land. The rewards of visiting begin even before you climb the 106 stone steps leading up to the outlook, as just the drive into the area is worth the time. Topographically speaking, it's here that the gentle prairies give way to the beloved Texas Hill Country. Austin is positioned on the eastern edge of this special region of the Lone Star State. The Hill Country is a respectable 4,350 miles in area and sits on top of Edwards Aquifer, the second-largest artisan water source on Earth.

Standing 785 feet tall, Mount Bonnell is the second-highest peak in Austin and the highest public viewing space available. If you've made it up to the top and are taking in the view, then below us and to the west, along this portion of the Lower Colorado River, we have Lake Austin and the sprawling arch of the Pennybacker Bridge carrying the drivers of Highway 360. Lake Austin is a man-made lake created by damming the river. It's preceded by Lake Travis even farther to the west, and it gives way to Lady Bird Lake in the center of town. The trio of lakes serves as a center of outdoor activity for the whole region; after all, we usually enjoy around three hundred sunny days a year. For motorized boating, head to Lake Travis or Lake Austin. Lady Bird Lake allows fishing trawlers, kayaks, canoes and other manually propelled boats, but you'll have to head out of town and upriver to do any water skiing. You'll notice that palatial mansions dot the hills around Mount Bonnell. Life above the lake is hard to beat, and for the right price, you, too, can join the ranks of the rich and famous.

Covert Park is the official name of this space, and that's to honor the gift of the land from the Covert family to the city in 1939. Mount Bonnell has naturally attracted picnickers and sightseers for as long as the area has hosted the Anglo settlers of the Texas frontier, but its importance and its history reach much further back. It's a story that is literally older than written words and even memory. The

Approximate map of the Texas Hill Country region.

indigenous peoples of what is now called Texas have always used this area as a path out of the hills and down into the Colorado River Valley. Here they could trade with other tribes and families under the shade of giant live oak trees and in the cool of the crystal-clear springs.

Archaeologists generally agree that humans have continually inhabited Texas in excess of fifteen thousand years. The same breathtaking beauty that draws more than fifty-five thousand new residents to Austin each year has drawn human life to these comfortable climes for longer than we can truly comprehend.

Returning to the view, find a good lookout spot toward the east, and you'll see Austin laid out before us. One of the most notable buildings to the north of downtown is the University of Texas at Austin tower. Then, following south, your view falls onto the seemingly ever-growing garden of skyscrapers in downtown Austin. For many years, there were rules governing a building's height and location so as not to obstruct the view of the capitol building's dome. Called "Capitol Viewing Corridors," these strict zoning rules limited where large buildings could be located. Since changes to that code have been made, nearly every possible lot that can be built on either now hosts or will soon host a high-rise building of one sort or another. Austin has been in a building boom since the year 2000 and shows no sign of slowing anytime soon. Why the rush to build? If predictions are correct, the city will be home to 4.5 million people by 2040, and they'll all need to live, work and play somewhere. Considering the 2000 U.S. census count for Austin's population was a mere 675,000 weird and wonderful Austinites, that's a whole lot of folks joining the party!

Following the skyline as it leaps over the river to the southern bank, you see the Gothic Revival–style towers of St. Edward's University in the distance to the south. Between downtown and those spires lies the funky, fun neighborhood known as the '04, a lively neighborhood that's full of stories, food, shopping, music and fun—and we'll wind our way through it all.

Now soak in that view and let's head down the hill. We have some stops to make on the way to town.

LAGUNA GLORIA

3809 West 35th Street
Our second stop is just down the hill, only a few steps away from the peacocks and koi ponds of Mayfield Park, and its name is Laguna Gloria.

Stephen F. Austin, Father of Texas and the first settler to claim the land around Laguna Gloria. *Courtesy of the Texas State Library and Archives Commission.*

This plot of land, just like Mount Bonnell and the adjacent park, has been welcoming humans for thousands of years. The original draw wasn't just its innate beauty, which it offers in spades, but especially tempting were the fresh cool springs that now run underground.

This land is so naturally alluring that Stephen F. Austin himself was the first to lay a claim on the property, back when the first settlers were exploring the farthest edge of the Texas frontier. Austin wrote in 1832 that he hoped to build a home on the site someday, though it would never come to pass. What we find here today is the hard work of a more modern effort made by Clara Driscoll and her husband, editor of the local *Austin American* newspaper Hal Sevier.

Clara was an amazing woman, and she left a huge legacy behind. Born to advantage and educated in private schools, she was a world-traveling polyglot who could converse in no fewer than four languages. By the time she was twenty-four years old, she and a friend from the newly formed Daughters of the Republic of Texas had led the effort to convince the State of Texas to purchase and preserve the Alamo—yes, *that* Alamo, which had been in private ownership and had sadly fallen into disrepair over the years.

The impact she would go on to have on the world didn't end there, and among many other things, later in life she would become the Democratic Party's national chairwoman for Texas. She held the post for sixteen years, from 1922 to 1938, and any politician of her time would learn to respect her, if not from her reputation then for her ability to out-drink and out-cuss any smoke-filled political back room from Texas to D.C.

Clearly, Clara was possessed with boundless energy. Besides her public efforts, the cultural expectations placed on her as a socialite and her passion for creating her amazing gardens, she still somehow found time for her own artistic pursuits as an author. She published two books and produced a three-act comic opera based on one of her books. *Mexicana* ran for eighty-two performances in New York City from January 29, 1906, until its curtain call on April 7, 1907. Clara wasn't just the producer, either. She even helped write the opera's lyrics.

Front yard sculpture garden at Laguna Gloria.

In 1943, Clara donated Laguna Gloria to the City of Austin to serve as a place where the public could interact with art, and by 1961, that dream was realized with the creation of the Laguna Gloria Art Museum. The museum soon began offering art classes as a side program, and by 1983, the popular art school had grown enough to warrant its own building on the site.

In 1992, the museum changed its name to the Austin Museum of Art. The program remained centered out of this space until the AMA decided to change its name to Contemporary Austin and soon moved its main operations to its new downtown location, the Contemporary Austin–Jones Center, in 2010. At the same time as the expansion to downtown, the show spaces at Laguna Gloria received a major remodel, and the facility began a new chapter as home to special gallery showings, with the always popular art school continuing on the grounds even today. It's perhaps on this point that Clara's greatest legacy lies, with the countless art students and visitors who have come to this long-revered space for inspiration and then taken that spark with them as they've gone back out into the world.

TEXAS MILITARY FORCES MUSEUM

2200 West 35th Street—Camp Mabry

Camp Mabry, situated at the base of Mount Bonnell, was established in 1892, making this the third-oldest active military installation in Texas. This post serves as the headquarters of the Texas Military Department and Texas Military Forces, and it's also the home to our next destination, the Texas Military Forces Museum (TMFM).

The TMFM has a mission: "To tell the story of the Texas Military forces from 1823 through the present and into the future." It does a fine job of it, with forty-five thousand square feet of indoor and outdoor galleries and over ten thousand artifacts. Included among the many sights are eight staggeringly detailed dioramas that bring to life important battles that Texas military forces have played a part in.

This museum doesn't hide its treasures, and as soon as you walk in, you'll be greeted by dozens of retired military vehicles that run the gamut from jeeps to jets, displayed all around and overhead in the main room. There are also extensive collections in adjoining rooms that focus on the various eras of Texas military history and include not only the hardware of war but also the fashion. Painstaking re-creations of the uniforms of the Republic of Texas military branches are on display. There's more than just the giant indoor space, though. Don't miss the extensive outdoor pieces included in the collection while you're there.

Admission is free, but since it's on an active military base, be sure to have your ID ready to be checked at the gate. For large group guided tours, call ahead, and for small groups, just ask for a docent-led tour from the information desk as you check in upon arrival.

PEASE PARK

1100 Kingsbury Street

For at least twelve thousand years, Shoal Creek has consistently remained an important part of life for humans living in this area. Archaeologists have since confirmed what the first Anglo settlers on the edge of the Texas frontier regularly reported: that large numbers of Indigenous people had long been utilizing the land around the creek, and its pristine water, to sustain their day-to-day needs. These reports continued beyond our days as the small frontier village of Waterloo and well into the time of the founding

Pease Park arched stone gate.

and construction of Austin. The proximity of the two very different worlds, Anglo and Indigenous, would prove catastrophic at times. Despite occasional glimpses of a possible coexistence, ultimately any agreements between the two peoples were abandoned, and all Native tribes, be they friend or foe, were pushed out of the area entirely.

Well before those relations would sour, the man who was sent to carve a capital city out of the farthest edge of the wilderness was Edwin Waller. This would be his toughest logistical challenge yet, but as a man endowed with managerial acumen, he was uniquely suited for the herculean task. The next closest piece of civilization was many miles downstream, at the small frontier town of Bastrop. Anything that you wanted to have at the new capital either had to be built on site from raw materials or brought in on a wagon from someplace very far away. Not to mention the fact that there was still a large, well-armed and determined Mexican army nearby. Also worth a second mention, of course, is the fact that the area was heavily populated by three different Indigenous tribes and that one of those three tribes was the much-feared Comanche. Being the designer and founder of the capital city of the new republic may someday hold honor, but getting it done was not an enviable task. Waller only had five months in which to go from forest and prairie to a functioning capital city, fully prepared to receive the new nation's most eminent politicians and heroes, all of whom would soon be heading to the new town for the next session of congress.

One benefit of planning a city is that you get to name everything, and Waller is said to have given this creek its name. A shoal being a shallow portion of a body of water, Shoal Creek must have seemed a perfectly reasonable name. Waller used the creek as the western edge of his city plan, and the creek that served as the new city's eastern border bore his name as Waller Creek. Working with what was already present, Waller chose a city plan laid out by nature. Shoal creek to the west, Waller Creek to the east, the Colorado River as a natural southern line and the prominent Capitol Hill, where the Texas State Capitol building now sits, was the boundary to the north. Nearly all the streets traveling east to west were named after trees, though that would change to a numeric system by the late 1800s, and nearly all of the streets traveling from north to south took on the names of rivers; for the most part, those streets still retain their original names.

By the 1850s, Texas had been annexed into the American Union and therefore was no longer at war with Mexico. With its southern flank secured, and with all traces of Native Americans gone from the area, Texas settlement of the Austin area expanded into the Shoal Creek Valley. In 1853, a large antebellum Greek Revival home was designed by master architect Abner H. Cook, the same man who also designed the Texas governor's mansion. The home was originally constructed on the 365-acre Woodlawn Plantation. In 1857, ownership of the property would transfer to three-time governor of Texas Elisha M. Pease and his wife, Lucadia. The portion of the plantation that is now Pease Park was always Lucadia's favorite part of the property, and she would often ride her carriage along Shoal Creek to take in the picturesque scene.

Governor Pease is one of many complicated characters who we'll come across in our exploration. He was elected to office twice before the Civil War, but when the rift between states broke out, he was known to be staunchly pro-Union, despite his ownership of slaves and the plantation where they labored without compensation on his behalf. His political stance was also very much in opposition to nearly all of his neighbors, friends and peers. The couple stayed in Austin throughout the Civil War but kept a low profile on the dinner party circuit.

With the South defeated, the Union needed to restore the rule of United States law, such as emancipation, in the cities of the South. When Union soldiers came to Austin for three months during Reconstruction, they were known to have set up camp in this area. One officer at that camp was none other than the infamous General Armstrong Custer. His Seventh Cavalry was among those troops stationed here, but they had a tough time of it. A cholera outbreak swept through the camp and left somewhere between thirty-five and forty of his soldiers dead. Today, Pease Park remembers that time by calling the area where they camped "Custer's Field."

Also during Reconstruction, Union general Philip Sheridan appointed Pease as the civilian governor of Texas in 1867, but with the staunch anti-Union sentiment of the time, his third term in office wasn't as well received as before. He decided to leave office early and resigned in 1869. Following his resignation, he and his wife traveled to the social circles of New England, and while there, they found a bit of inspiration in the new City Beautiful movement that was spawning grand public spaces such as New York City's Central Park and Prospect Park in Brooklyn. When the couple returned to life in Texas, they decided to donate a portion of their own land to Austin for use as our first park so that Austinites could also enjoy nature while still in the city.

In 1952, Janet Long Fish made the next major contribution to the park by convincing the city to approve construction of the nation's first hike and bike trail, which is still a major attraction to this day. Janet laid out the path herself, but being a bit on the shorter side, she had to walk ahead of the machinery, in weeds that reached above her head, and throw her hat up to let the workers driving the bulldozer know which way to go. The trail she blazed was more than just through the weeds of Pease Park, and her idea would go on to inspire countless other cities around the world to create their own trail systems in the decades to come.

With the park well established, it began to host special events, but one of those annual gatherings surpasses all the rest. That event is none other than Eeyore's Birthday. Yes, the beloved if beleaguered donkey from *Winnie the Pooh*. This Austin tradition benefiting children's charities eventually outgrew its original home, and in 1974, the party moved here. Eeyore's birthday is a very special, and very Austin, event. It's sort of a bohemian celebration of springtime and of life. It's a costume party, so make sure you dress up. If you have kiddos, be sure to come early. There's a maypole wrapping ceremony and other special family-friendly events to enjoy in the first half of the day. The event is free, and all the money that's raised through concessions and donations is sent to a litany of good causes centered on children and their needs. Check out the event's website for more detailed information.

Statue of Eeyore at Eastwood Park in Austin, the original home of Eeyore's Birthday Party.

The history of Pease Park is far deeper than the water of Shoal Creek, but its future is bright indeed with the addition of several new features to the park, including pavilions, performance spaces, art installations and recreational features, as well as increasing and improving the beloved hike and bike trail. Whether you come for one of the big parties, to take a nice stroll through the sculpture garden or to fly that new kite, Pease Park has many things to offer and certainly something for just about anyone, including any would-be treasure hunters.

THE LOST TREASURE OF SHOAL CREEK

The story of the lost treasure of Shoal Creek comes to us from one of Austin's most colorful and revered residents, William Sydney Porter. He was known to his friends as Bill but known to the world as the master of short stories and sudden plot twists, O. Henry. Bill Porter moved to Austin as a young man in 1885. This was an exciting era for a town that was full of opportunity and bursting with growth. When he arrived, the capitol building was being replaced by the granite behemoth that we see today. The sight of its famed dome nearing completion on Capitol Hill must have lent an air of promise to the moment. As with many of Austin's imported residents, Bill knew upon his very first visit that he wanted to live here and moved right in.

Bill Porter was a bright, talented and charismatic fellow. A capable man, he worked a variety of jobs, and his connections would open doors for him along the way. No matter what was going on in his life, the one constant for him was always the writing that would persistently consume his passions. In the end, those odd jobs along the way would also frequently provide him with the source material for his many stories. This is a pattern that holds true for our legendary lost treasure, as he claims that he was first told the story while visiting with an old shepherd during his work drawing up county maps for the state's General Land Office.

According to the story, as a young boy, one of the men in this shepherd's little village would occasionally tell stories about the war with Texas. The man said that in 1836, while in the Mexican army, he was one of a small group of soldiers secretly recruited to rob a pay wagon. The gold was meant to cover six months of overdue salaries for the soldiers of Santa Anna's army, deployed out in Mexico's northern frontier and fighting with the Texan rebels.

Under the direction of the paymaster, and with the collusion of a high-ranking general, the pay wagon turned north just before reaching the rear of the army, which was marching near San Antonio. When the wagon was safely off the path and nowhere near any major settlements, they set up camp to rest for the night. The storyteller and one other soldier saw an opportunity, made a pact and killed the rest of their party in their sleep. The man recounted how they took a jar and filled it with the blood of their victims, buried the treasure next to a creek near the Colorado River and, in a final gruesome act, poured the blood they'd collected over the treasure. This was a dark way to conjure and control a ghostly guardian that would watch over their ill-gotten gains until they could retrieve it.

A cyclist entering the downtown segment of the Shoal Creek Trail.

Finally, they carved eagle wings into a nearby live oak tree to serve as a marker on their treasure map.

With the hard work done, the storyteller then admitted that he killed his partner, the sole witness, so he could claim the treasure for himself once the theft had been forgotten. Not sure what else to do in the meantime, the man said he returned to the army amid the confusion of battle and ultimately returned to his village in Mexico where he'd live to tell the tale. The general who was in on the caper was said to have been slain in one of the battles against the Texans, leaving the murderer as the only person to know the truth about the caper. This soldier who had succumbed to greed and killed so many men to hide this treasure had never gotten over his fear of punishment if he was caught with the gold. He never attempted to reclaim it, so the treasure surely remained in the same spot where it was buried.

The shepherd commented to Bill that the soldier was now dead but that he still knew the man's son. For $100, he would go to Mexico, secure the map and return it to Porter in Austin, where he would help once more by translating the map. Bill was short on money but gave the man the only $20 he had, right then and there, and they agreed the rest of the tab would be settled upon delivery. Porter's business partners and friends thought him a fool, but Bill believed in the validity of the tale and in the trustworthiness of his new acquaintance. He was confident that in no time he would find the treasure.

Months passed without word, until one day a letter came from a public scribe in Mexico reporting on behalf of the illiterate shepherd. The map had been found, and it could be brought to Austin, but the shepherd had taken ill during the journey and wouldn't be able to make the trip back. He was willing to send his son in his stead with the map, and the son would also be able to decipher and translate it. The only catch, of course, was funding. To proceed any further, forty-five dollars had to be sent post haste, but the remaining sum of thirty-five dollars could be settled upon delivery. Bill didn't hesitate to send the funds despite the jeers from his business partners, two brothers by the names of Dixie and Vic Daniels, who thought scraping up the money to buy a newspaper (as planned) would be a much wiser investment.

More time passed, and a few months later, a young man from Mexico came to town asking for Bill Porter. It was the shepherd's son; he had come with the map, and he meant to make good on his father's deal. With the freshly interpreted directions in hand, they set about homing in on where to begin their hunt. Eventually, they realized the treasure must lie somewhere along the banks of Shoal Creek and was likely to be found just west of Capitol Hill. Now all they had to do was locate the live oak tree with the eagle's wings carved into its bark so many years ago. After carefully scanning over the bark of every tree along the creek, they found one that, if you squinted and tilted your head just right, seemed to possibly have the remnants of a mark that could have once been in the shape of wings. Certainly, it was their best bet, and considering how much a tree could have changed in appearance over the sixty years between the burial and the hunt for treasure, they convinced themselves that they'd found it.

Bill and the Daniels brothers rented a heavy-duty wagon to haul their would-be treasure. They gathered some shovels and lanterns and some pistols—just in case—and waited for the cover of dark.

Once the men were sure that enough of the town had retired to their respective homes for the night, they set out for the creek. Between the map's directions and Bill's foresight of asking a local geology professor just how much soil would have accumulated along the creek over the course of sixty years, the crew felt confident that the treasure should be just five and a half feet below ground. They set into digging at once, and the first foot of soil was compact and hard to dig, just as the geologist predicted. Beyond that first foot of earth, the soil seemed somewhat easier to cut into, as if it had already once been disturbed. The group fervently agreed among themselves that the section of ground that was anomalous was in just the right dimensions to hold a large chest, too. There was excitement on the site. Surely, they were just moments from their prize! Farther and farther down they dug, and at the five-foot mark, just before they could claim their reward, they heard an ungodly screeching. A howling, shrieking scream bellowed down the creek bed. They lit lanterns in a hurry, and shovels were discarded in favor of their pistols. What sort of banshee could this be? Was the cursed ghostly guardian of the treasure upon them? After too long for comfort, the screaming stopped. The tense moments of silence passed slowly, but soon enough the gold lust returned. Lanterns off, voices down, shovels out, they started to dig. No more had they put blade to earth when the shrieking returned. That was enough to send them running, all hopes of fortune abandoned in the protection of their lives, if not their very souls.

The next day's newspapers mentioned nothing about the treasure hunt or its untimely conclusion, but there was a story that gave Bill and his friends reason to pause. Apparently, an inmate of the local insane asylum had escaped and was found shrieking and running up and down Shoal Creek at just the time the crew had experienced their haunting. They must have been relieved by their folly and emboldened to resume the hunt. Silly superstitions wouldn't get the best of this intrepid group, and they vowed to return that evening for one more go at the lost treasure.

The men gathered at the site, wielded their shovels, dug the last six inches and found…bedrock. No treasure, no gold, no curse—not a thing. Nothing but the limestone the city stands on. With that, they retired from the treasure-hunting business and relieved themselves of their quest and their shovels, and Porter got back to a writer's life in bustling Austin.

Being such a renowned fiction author, there's every chance that this whole tale was an entertaining invention of William Sydney Porter. However, the greatest fictions come from a seed of truth, and this is not the only legend that's been told of treasure hastily cached along Shoal Creek. There's also a story of Spanish conquistadors hiding silver and gemstones from the Comanches. Another tale has Confederate soldiers hurriedly moving the riches of Texas to a spot along the creek to keep it from the Union soldiers who were closing in on the city. Whether the wealth of treasure stories in the area gives O. Henry's tale an air of credence, or whether it casts a shadow of doubt on the subject, it is interesting to consider an article written in 1927 that was printed in an area newspaper of the time called the *Rising Star Record*. According to the report, an unidentified group of men labored for eight months on what would ultimately be a forty-foot tunnel along the bank of Shoal Creek. When questioned by the occasional curious passerby, one excuse or other was given to explain away the work site, pretending to be constructing the foundation of a bridge or laying the foundation work of a fine home being built for an anonymous patron. When these men weren't digging and blasting away at the tunnel, they kept a constant guard on the site, which was also curious to the townsfolk. Ultimately, on April 13 of that year, the mystery men must have found their quarry. The *Rising Star Record* reports, "A box was lifted from the square cut chamber between the rocks, for the next day the workmen were gone, and the blasting has ceased. Curious throngs of Austinites soon found the dark tunnel, and with lights, discovered traces of the large wooden box that had laid beneath the dirt for more than 60 years." Curiouser and curiouser. Perhaps there really was once a treasure along Shoal Creek after all.

THE TREATY OAK

507 Baylor Street
Departing Pease Park via Lamar Boulevard, we next travel a few blocks south. Tucked a block away from the crowds at the Whole Foods world headquarters is a hidden gem of Texas history. It's a stately Texas live oak tree that, if we're being honest, looks a little bit lopsided. After you've heard the story of this grand old tree, you might just forgive its look and not judge this tree by its bark alone.

For more than five hundred years, the Treaty Oak has stood proud and drawn people to its shade. It's the last surviving member of what was once a grouping of fourteen trees called Council Grove. The last of her sisters fell to a flood in the early 1900s, but this tree has gone on strong ever since.

Council Grove long served as a sacred space for the Tonkawa and Comanche tribes. Not only was it the site for the talks and ceremonies of both war and peace, but its acorns were used to brew a tea drank by tribal women. This tea provided the women with a way to channel the energy of the tree and send strength and comfort to loved ones away on long journeys or off in battle.

Local, potentially apocryphal lore also holds that the Treaty Oak was the site of the first boundary agreement ever negotiated between Texan settlers and the local Native tribes. Imagine it's 1824; the whole area is untamed and unspoiled frontier, and it's years before the dream of a Lone

The beloved and historic Treaty Oak, a Texas live oak tree standing in one-third of its former glory after surviving an attack with poison.

Star Republic would be realized. Under these very branches, the father of Texas, Stephen F. Austin, is said to have negotiated a fragile peace with the Indigenous tribes who had called this land home since time immemorial.

In March 1861, the drums of the Civil War and secession were pounding from all corners of this newly annexed state. Despite strong protest from staunchly pro-Union governor Sam Houston, Texans chose to join the Confederacy and booted Houston out of office. Dejected and furious, he's said to have stormed out of the capitol and walked to this tree. Here he sat, resting his back on its trunk, and considered not just his fate but also the fate of the whole nation.

This tree is more than just historic; it's biologically perfect. It's a dendrologist's dream and an arborist's pin-up! In its prime, the Treaty Oak was regarded by the American Forestry Association as "the most perfect specimen of any living tree in the country," and its photograph hangs in that group's hall of fame. With all of this positive attention, it makes sense that in 1936, the City of Austin would take over stewardship of the land the oak sits on and create a park to protect the tree from the rapid development of the area.

In 1989, the story of the Treaty Oak took a bizarre twist when the tree was intentionally poisoned with enough of the hardwood herbicide Velpar to kill one hundred lesser trees. There was a huge outpouring of support for the tree, as well as understandable anger over the assault on both the tree and Texas history. Dupont Chemical offered up $10,000 in reward money to help find the perpetrator, and eccentric Texan billionaire Ross Perot offered a blank check to save the tree.

The restoration efforts from the experts included soil replacement, sugar doses to the root system and the installation of a spring water misting system. Efforts on the part of the community at large included hand-drawn cards from the schoolkids, flowers, crystals, prayer, group meditation and, of course, psychic healing ceremonies. We'll never know if it was the intensive care of the highly trained arborists or the crystals and psychic healing that did the trick, or perhaps a combination of both, but after some time, the tree was stabilized. The once proud 127-foot crown was reduced by half from precision pruning, and in the end, two-thirds of the tree would die, but overall, the tree was saved.

Later, a man whose disturbing demeanor drew skeptical attention was bragging in a local bar about having been the vandal of the Treaty Oak. He boasted about how he poisoned the tree as a way to cast a powerful dark magic spell. He was quickly turned over to police by his fellow bar patrons, and following an arrest and trial, the man spent nine years in prison for his conviction of felony criminal mischief.

It's true that the tree is a shadow of its former glory, but any history lover appreciates the scars from battles won. Consider all it's been through and all that it has meant to so many different kinds of people who lived in so many eras in time. Take into account the fact that it still stands majestic in its own lopsided way despite all the world has thrown at it, and when you do, you'll surely agree that the Treaty Oak remains the perfect specimen of any tree.

CLARKSVILLE HISTORIC DISTRICT

Continuing west on 6th Street takes us deeper into a very historic neighborhood in Austin called Clarksville. Founded in 1871 by freedman

Charles Clark, this is the oldest surviving freedmen's colony "west of the Mississippi River," which is always a favorite colloquial measurement.

Clark was born under enslavement in 1820, and according to available sources, he likely came to Texas around 1850. After emancipation, he purchased two acres of land from a former Confederate general and one-time Austin mayor, Nathan Shelley, for $100. He soon built a home for his family on land that would one day be considered West 10th Street. Clark would sell off smaller plots of his two acres to other families, creating the seeds of community as his tradition dictated. Soon, other freedmen bought the nearby adjacent plots that had once been the site of the Pease Plantation prior to the Civil War.

In no time, Clarksville was up and running, situated safely beyond the western edge of town. Soon, as was intended, a thriving community of people no longer bound by slavery was springing up around Mr. Clark. By 1882, the Sweet Home Missionary Baptist Church, which still operates today, had opened its doors, and as early as 1890, the Clarksville school was in operation and serving the neighborhood children.

In the early 1900s, European immigrants were moving into Clarksville, which was quickly becoming a vibrant, multiracial community just outside town. Before the segregation laws of the Jim Crow era had even taken effect, real estate developers had their eye on this well-positioned neighborhood that was once fully separate from Austin but was now suddenly attractively close to the expanding downtown district. The steadily increasing pressure on these homeowners to give up their land began as early as a decade before the laws in Austin were altered to enforce racial segregation. For example, the Austin school board closed the Clarksville school in 1918 as a way to limit city-funded support for the freedmen's colony.

In 1928, Austin sought and put into action a systemic segregation plan that placed enormous pressure on the Black population of Austin to relocate to the only place the law would allow them to live. This is the area that we now call East Austin. We'll delve more into this incredibly impactful policy when we explore that section of the city.

When the laws changed to force removal, the people of Clarksville refused to abandon their homes. The tactic of cutting off social services increased as "all facilities and services" would be given only to Black residents living in the prescribed zone. This really meant that outside East Austin, city services such as gas or electricity, plumbing or trash collection would be physically removed or simply never offered to the Black residents of these neighborhoods in the first place. Still, the

Left: Historical marker commemorating Clarksville, one of Austin's original freedmen's colonies and the only one to survive outside the city-sanctioned segregated lines.

Below: Clarksville's Sweet Home Missionary Baptist Church, founded in 1871.

people of this district would choose to keep their homes and endure the indignities, such as the flooding creeks filled with sewage and the dirt roads that the city refused to pave.

In 1965, in an attempt to let progress do what laws seemingly could not, city planners steered the construction of the Loop 1/MOPAC Highway controversially through the middle of this hold-out freedmen's neighborhood, and in the process, 64 out of 168 houses were lost to the construction, displacing more than two hundred Black residents at the time. Still, those who could remain in the neighborhood did so.

For decades after the official end of Jim Crow laws, the kerosene lamps of Clarksville continued to be the only light available in some houses that sat along those crumbling roads, and the forsaken state of the district continued well into 1975. It was around this time that the city leaders gave up on trying to force the practices long known to be unconstitutional and that, as the years marched on, became viewed more often in white society as unseemly, if not morally reprehensible. Times they were a changing, and in 1976, the neighborhood received inclusion in the National Register of Historic Places and the City of Austin, with pressure from civic organizations, began pumping money into the long-ignored neighborhood. Throughout it all, the proud residents of Clarksville resisted the pressure to move, and it was the only freedmen's colony outside of East Austin to survive into the twentieth century.

The people who first called Clarksville home built up this beautiful neighborhood with their own hands, on land they had legally purchased and with money they were finally able to earn for themselves. At one point, there were as many as six freedmen's colonies around Austin, and over time nearly all of them would be forced out of their homes, with the exceptions of the colony at the heart of the new district reserved for people of color in East Austin and here in Clarksville. The actions of the past still impact the people of this city today, and we struggle with the realities of a history stained with racism. Today, we strive to create a place where our entire community can thrive while experiencing acceptance and living in abundance.

SOUTH AUSTIN

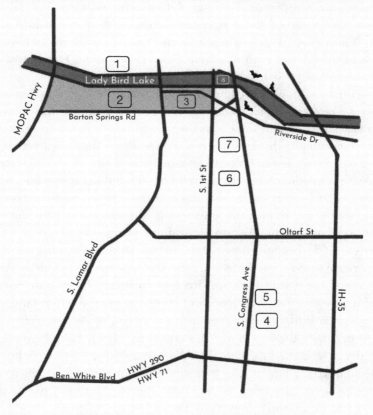

1.LadyBird Lake
2.Zilker Park
3.Auditorium Shores
4.Penn Field

5.St Edwards University
6.SoCo
7.Texas School for the Deaf
8.Gov Ann Richards Bridge

LADY BIRD LAKE

First things first, let's just get some FAQs out of the way. Yes, it's a lake, and yes, it's a river. Yes, it's the Colorado River. No, it's not *that* Colorado River.

Colorado means "red" or "reddish" in Spanish, and it's just as apt a description for the river that snakes through 862 miles of Texas as it is for the river out west that shares its name. That's a lot of river, and in fact, the Lower Colorado is the longest river to have both its source and its mouth within our state lines. Along the way, Texans have created many reservoirs and lakes from its water. Often referred to as the Highland lakes, we find three of these man-made bodies of water in and around Austin. The order of appearance as the river flows from northwest to southeast through our region is, first, Lake Travis; next, Lake Austin; and last, in town, Lady Bird Lake.

Lady Bird Lake was created in 1960 with the construction of the Longhorn Dam on the city's east side. The 416-acre site was known for many decades as "Town Lake" and was originally created to serve as the cooling reservoir for the Holly Street Power Plant that ran from 1960 to 2007. Put simply, Town Lake wasn't built with the city's enjoyment in mind. With no dedicated paths or parks for the public to use, and no civic engagement to keep it clean, this once under-appreciated watering hole became little more than a place for trash to collect and was often sadly referred to locally as the "Eyesore" for many years.

The year 1971 brought new public interest to the lake, and that's when the first push to do something with the site was spearheaded by Roberta Crenshaw, of the Austin Park and Recreation Board. They purchased and planted nearly four hundred trees and shrubs to get the ball rolling. At the same time, Roy Butler used his two terms as mayor of Austin, from 1971 to 1975, to persuade the city council to create the Town Lake Beautification Committee. He knew just who should serve as the committee's honorary chairperson: Mrs. Claudia Alta Johnson—also known as Lady Bird. Along with her personal donation of $19,000, she also brought much-needed attention and fundraising prowess to the committee.

The lake is now named for Lady Bird Johnson, of course, who was first lady of the United States and wife to Lyndon Baines Johnson. When not in Washington, D.C., Lady Bird and LBJ lived in the Austin area, and their influence is noted all over the region. She was always a big presence in the city, and Austin was often the beneficiary of her lifelong mission to beautify the world around her. She refused the honor of having the lake bear her

Texas
Highland
Lakes

Above: A pedestrian bridge spans busy Barton Creek, looking toward Lady Bird Lake.

Left: Approximate map of the Texas Highland lakes of the Lower Colorado River. Not included: Lake Austin and Lady Bird Lake.

name while she was alive, but just weeks after her death in 2007, the city council voted to change the name to Lady Bird Lake. Without her there to argue the point, the new name was adopted.

It would be hard to overstate the importance of Lady Bird Lake and the parks that surround it these days. Culturally speaking, Austin is an outdoors town, a point that bears repeating through these pages. Getting out to explore and enjoy the public spaces such as the lake, Zilker Park, Auditorium Shores and the hike and bike trails that connect it all and attending the many events that take place at these locations are major elements of our present zeitgeist.

As mentioned in the beginning of this adventure, boats on Lady Bird Lake tend to be manually operated since there's a ban on using anything bigger than a fishing trawler motor. The lack of a constant wake makes this lake a paradise for canoeing, kayaking and, ever popular in Austin, paddle board yoga. If you're visiting town and forgot to pack your kayak, rest assured that there are several rental options available on the lake. Aside from motors, swimming is also banned in the lake, so the connecting creeks, nearby springs and the pools they create are the places to find if you need a dip. With the high temperatures and high humidity present in Austin for nearly half the year, you'll not be faulted if you find yourself skipping ahead to the section of this book that covers Barton Springs.

ZILKER METROPOLITAN PARK

2100 Barton Springs Road
Welcome to Zilker Park—350 acres of all the fun situated right in the middle of Austin! Along with Lady Bird Lake, Zilker Park and the many activities that are held here serve as no less than the heart and soul of activity in Austin. Swimming, kayaking and canoeing, sand volleyball, basketball, a full eighteen-hole disc golf course, "polo fields" available for all manner of intramural or casual Saturday afternoon sport, miles of hike and bike trails, a sculpture garden, a botanical garden, a theater, picnic spaces, gigantic music festivals and, of course, so many stories await you here.

BARTON SPRINGS

2113 William Barton Drive

Stephen F. Austin's second group of colonizers had among its ranks three brothers by the surname of Barton, and one of those brothers would go on to leave an indelible mark on our city. In 1828, William Barton, or Billie to his friends, lost his young bride soon after giving birth to their only child. That's when he decided to join his brothers with his young daughter and five slaves he'd inherited from his father and take a gamble on the move to Texas. What drives a man to abandon civilization, to risk life and limb on the edge of the world? Ultimately, it was the age-old hope for some peace and quiet. It's unlikely that Billie found much of either, but he did find adventure, and in the process, he built a legend for himself as no less than the "Daniel Boone of Texas."

By all accounts, it seems just about all Billie wanted at first was solitude. He once served as a mid-level political representative for his community when it was his turn to shoulder the hassle, but he was an independent loner

Kayakers, paddleboarders and swimmers enjoy Barton Creek.

by nature, and in the early 1830s, he thought he'd finally found a spot near Bastrop to homestead where he'd be left alone to farm and raise cattle. It was a reasonable assumption; after all, he was on the edge of the Texas frontier. Alas, the frontier never stays that way for long. Eventually, someone decided to move within ten miles of him, and when he saw the smoke from their campfire, he knew it was time to pull up stakes and push upriver.

Barton landed forty-five miles north, in a gorgeous spot on what was actually the southern edge of the Comanche Nation. Unwelcome and uninvited by the Indigenous people, he would be one of the first Anglo settlers to call this area home. The Comanches had been expanding their control over most of the southwest portion of what is now the United States for more than one hundred years. Having mastered the horses brought to the Americas by the early Spanish explorers, the Comanche left their ancestral homes in the Rocky Mountains and spread their culture through the plains and then south toward Mexico. Regardless of any claims by Spain, Mexico or Texas, it was this fearsome tribe that had been the law and the ruling power in this particular area for the thirty years prior to Barton's arrival. The Tonkawa and the Apache Lupin still lived in the area, but the Comanche were in control. Barton would spend the next ten years fighting tooth and nail to keep his life and his claimed land. He may have temporarily succeeded in leaving most of the Anglo world behind, but Billie Barton was hardly alone. Through the struggle, he carved his legend as a tough-as-nails pioneer and an "Indian killer."

By 1837, the settlement called Waterloo was slowly building up around Barton, and this time, he was apparently unwilling to push deeper into the frontier. Perhaps the one thing that kept him around is that he'd met his second wife, Stacey Pryor, and together they'd have three daughters.

Barton built his new family a home on the edge of the Hill Country, which the folks of the time referred to as the mountains. Indeed, without our modern vehicles and roads, these hills might seem more like mountains to us, too. Most importantly, the land includes three big cool springs that feed into a clear, broad creek that, in turn, spills out into the Colorado River. It has to be noted that this land and these springs were frequently visited by, and long considered sacred to, those three local tribes just mentioned. As a result, Barton would find himself involved in even more clashes over the years to come.

The threat to settlers was eliminated once and for all with the removal of these Indigenous people from Texas, and Austin was starting to thrive and expand beyond its original boundaries. Barton, or Uncle Billie, as he was known to folks in this era, was now living a much less antisocial existence with his growing lot of new neighbors and a large family running around him. In fact, he named the three springs on his property after his three young daughters—Eliza, Parthenia and Zenobia—and opened up access to his land to let swimmers, toe dippers, parched travelers and even passing cattle herds, allowing all to find refreshment from its waters.

This idea of allowing access to the springs would become somewhat of an unspoken tradition with every owner of the land. The Rabb family purchased the plot from the Barton family in the 1860s and still welcomed visitors, while also running a water mill on the site. They sold it to someone else who again permitted swimming, but they also built an ice factory on the property. That ice factory, though not originally built by him, would ultimately become synonymous with a man named Andrew Jackson Zilker.

Zilker came to Austin as a young man with fifty cents in his pocket. He also had big dreams of building his fortune and had the flash of ambition in his eyes. He first worked a series of seemingly random jobs, advancing and making connections along way. Zilker was always civically minded, which led him to become a founding member of the Elks Lodge in town. Not long after the lodge was formed, he took work as a laborer at the newly built ice factory. With the help of his influential brethren, he quickly rose up the ranks to foreman and then became owner of not just the factory but also the land it sat upon and the springs that fed it. This enormous windfall and rise in station all occurred in a matter of months, reminding us that it can truly pay to have influential friends. He'd go on to leverage the success of that ice factory into other businesses, ultimately becoming one of Austin's first millionaires. Once Zilker had secured his fortune, he turned his considerable energy toward his interest in civic duty and served as the chairman of the public school board.

It was during his time leading the school system that Zilker came up with a way to create stability for the local educational system and at the same time see to it that the people of Austin would get to enjoy the springs and the land around them for generations to come. He would offer to sell this prime land to the city on the condition that it become a public park and use the proceeds from the sales to endow a trust that would fund public education in the city. Zilker was quoted saying, "Barton Springs is a sacred spot. It would be a wrongful thing for this beauty spot to be owned by any individual. It ought to belong to all the people of Austin." In 1934, the city officially named the space Zilker Park, and of course, we still call this pool Barton Springs.

AZIE MORTON ROAD

The name of the street that takes us to Austin's favorite summertime haunt is Azie Morton Road. Long before her name replaced Robert E. Lee Drive in 2018, Azie Taylor Morton had already made a splash at Barton Springs. To begin this tale with her meaningful dive in 1961 would be to do an injustice to her larger story. If we take a moment to put her act of defiance into the context of her life up to that point, a richer character will come into view.

Azie was a Black woman born near tiny Dale, Texas, to Fleta Hazel Taylor in 1936. Though quite capable in most respects, Fleta was both deaf and mute. Her daughter Azie was born as healthy and capable as any mother could dream. She lacked any hearing issues and by all accounts was a normal, curious and bright child. Azie attended primary school in Dale, but this was the height of the Jim Crow era with its segregation laws, and there were no high schools near her hometown that would allow Black students at the time. Not one to be deterred, Azie would find her path to higher education by moving to Austin alone to attend high school at the Texas School for the Deaf. She spent her entire childhood surrounded by people of all races and born of all classes, burdened with the real, lifelong obstacles of physical limitation and the burdens of societal bigotry regardless of their race. Yet somehow, impossibly, she also witnessed them overcoming those challenges daily. It's easy to imagine Azie taking from her childhood a special and deeply held inspiration to always keep pushing forward and not allow life's many roadblocks to keep her from doing what she wanted to do with her time on earth.

Azie excelled at her studies while living at the School for the Deaf, and though she graduated from high school early, she still wasn't finished educating herself. In 1952, she was accepted to Huston-Tillotson, a historically Black university in East Austin. Azie's studious nature persisted, and she performed well in college, too. Once she'd earned her undergraduate degree, Azie applied to the University of Texas at Austin to pursue her master's degree.

In those years, which marked the beginnings of the civil rights era, Black students were occasionally, if rarely, allowed to attend the master's programs at UT Austin. Black students were not, however, allowed to attend any undergraduate courses. When Azie applied for grad school, she was told that she lacked certain credits that could only be obtained by attending additional undergrad classes on the UT Austin campus but that the school rules would not allow her to attend those classes because of her race. Though she would have preferred to have continued on with college, she was caught in a racially charged catch-22.

Always looking forward, Azie left academia and joined the workforce. In the summer of 1961, while working as a secretary, Azie met and became friends with the founding editor of the *Texas Observer*, Ronnie Dugger. He was a young, bright, ambitious writer looking to carve out his place in the community. This was at the height of a moment when on any given summer day at Barton Springs, mixed in with all the other (white) Austinites out in the sun were all the great minds and leaders of the city. These men of renown would regularly make their appearances beside the pool and hold court at their chosen spot surrounded by their fans and disciples. It was the epicenter of recreation for the wealthy socialites of the elite class, as well as the common man. So, like everyone else, Ronnie and his family would swim there almost daily.

It bears noting that for the bulk of its history, the springs and the creek were open to anyone regardless of their skin color. All of that changed when the city began building infrastructure on the site, starting with that pavilion that was all the rage in the Roaring Twenties. From then on, it was no longer accessible to anyone other than whites. This harsh reality of racial segregation was pervasive in every aspect of life in the capital city, and the removal of access to natural recreational spaces was an especially tough blow to communities of color. As the seeds of the civil rights movement started to take root across America, it was the deeply human desire to freely enjoy those long beloved natural spaces that most fervently fueled the passions of the local protests for equal rights and equal access in Austin. This issue of segregated parks became the focus of the local activists.

Two years before the 1963 marches, Azie was chatting with Ronnie one afternoon in her office. The topic of Barton Springs and segregation came up, and the two decided they would no longer just wait for the laws of the land or the hearts of the locals to change. Instead, they'd integrate Barton Springs themselves. Azie would just walk down there and go swimming, and Ronnie would go with her. They saw no reason to complicate things by making a fuss or asking for permission. Azie, Ronnie and his family went down to the springs the next day. Azie, wearing a lovely white bathing suit that shined against her dark black skin, walked up to the edge of the pool. It's said she looked like a magazine model as she did a perfect dive into the sixty-eight-degree water, accompanied by sounds of gasps and the not so hushed mutterings of the offended white socialites sitting in their favorite spots nearby. After some time in the pool, Azie Taylor Morton and the

Dugger family relaxed on their towels and soaked in the sun. Soon, another white woman in attendance quietly stood up, walked over to their spot and joined them, offering a silent but clear show of support. The splash was heard all over town, and with all that watering and all that sunshine, the seeds of integration were now sprouting above the soil. Many individuals and organizations would come together in the years that followed to bring the segregation of Austin parks to an end. It was a long and often contentious process, but the grassroots campaign spawned the 1963 protest marches in Austin that brought the change in the city policy that would finally allow for integration, first in the parks and then in all public spaces.

Azie went on to lead a rich and notable life. She cut her political teeth helping with LBJ's senatorial campaigns; Kennedy asked her to be a part of the Equal Employment Committee; and then she served as the first Black female United States treasurer for the Carter administration. As U.S. treasurer, her signature was, for a time, emblazoned onto every bit of currency guaranteed by the United States.

Azie Taylor Morton is known for carving out a special place for herself in history, and she would open many doors for those who would come behind her. Along the way, her work ethic and indomitable spirit would earn her many admirers and friends. One of those friends was another trailblazer and leader of the civil rights movement, Barbra Jordan. She was not only the first Black woman to be elected to Congress in the U.S. House of Representatives, but Jordan also went on to become the first person of color to serve in the Texas Senate since the Reconstruction era and the first Black woman to ever serve in that body. At Azie's Treasury swearing-in ceremony, Senator Jordan said of her friend, "She may not have intended to be an example to others—but became an example. Her life is a manual on how to succeed by trying. It is a certification of the rewards of hard work and competence." It seems like not taking "No" for an answer was a big part of Azie's secret recipe, too.

JAPANESE ZEN GARDEN AT ZILKER BOTANICAL GARDEN

2220 Barton Springs Road

Just west of the polo fields and picnic tables of Zilker Park is a very special place. Find the tree-covered hill, take the gated entrance inside and behold: the Zilker Botanical Gardens. It is unique for having been born of six different gardening clubs in the 1960s and has now grown to thirty clubs with over 1,500 members. All of these groups have banded together for the

The koi ponds spell "Austin" in the Japanese Zen Garden at Zilker Botanical Garden.

central purpose of creating Austin's own grand public gardens, managed under the unifying umbrella of the Austin Area Garden Center, a nonprofit that raises funds to maintain the grounds for its more than 300,000 annual visitors to enjoy.

Tucked inside this enchanted space is the Isamu Taniguchi Japanese Garden, which opened to the public a few years into the life of the Zilker Botanical Garden, in 1969. This addition was the creation of one man toiling mostly alone for eighteen months to transform a steep, barren, caliche-covered hillside into one of Austin's favorite and most serene environs. It was built with no more of a plan than a sketch because, as "Old Man Taniguchi" liked to teach people, the garden reveals itself. Oh, and it bears mentioning that the man behind this botanical masterpiece was nearly seventy years old when he began the behemoth effort.

What would possess a man to spend his retirement performing such backbreaking work? The answer lies in Mr. Taniguchi's story. Born in 1897 in Japan, which at the time was a nation that only then was emerging from more than two thousand years of extreme cultural isolationism, Isamu immigrated with his family to America in 1914 when he was seventeen years old. Living in California, he embraced his new home and became a successful tenant farmer, created a thriving co-op and was even part of the effort to create a new tomato that would survive the trip from the West Coast to the East Coast. Life was good, and the Taniguchis (he'd made a family with his lifelong love by then) were living out the American dream. That dream, like so many of the sweetest ones, came to an abrupt and bitter end.

World War II was raging, and anti-Japanese fever was sweeping America. One day, the authorities came knocking down Isamu's door and informed him that he had three hours to pack a single bag, say goodbye to his family and report for detention as an "enemy alien." After some jail time and some time spent bouncing between detention camps, the Taniguchi family was finally able to reunite at the Crystal City internment camp in the Rio Grande Valley of Texas. During this time, the two sons of the family had grown to fighting age, and instead of attending college as planned, they were drafted into the military where they and some 4,000 other Japanese American young men were asked to fight for a country that was at the same time detaining more than 120,000 of their kin in concentration camps.

The sons did their part for the war effort, and when hostilities ended, the family was eventually released and reunited. The sons went on to attend and receive degrees from UT Austin. One of the boys, Alan, got a degree in architecture specializing in landscape design. With his credentials, he found work that led him to design the city's prized hike and bike trails around Lady Bird Lake. Meanwhile, Mr. Taniguchi stayed in the Rio Grande Valley and farmed in the area until he retired.

Mr. Taniguchi was encouraged by his sons to join them in Austin for his golden years, and he agreed, but he must have found retirement too relaxing. He was in real need of a project that was bigger than him, and Alan used his connections with the parks department to find just the right place for Isamu to work some magic on a barren hill on the edge of the city's new botanical garden.

On one level, Isamu Taniguchi saw his garden as an opportunity to thank the city that educated his sons and adopted him in his retirement. More than that, he also knew that after the long and brutal war, Japanese culture had a gift it could give the world that could help everyone find peace: their traditional meditation gardens. By creating this garden, he was creating a bridge between cultures and helping to heal deeply felt societal wounds. Amid the waterfalls and the koi ponds—one of which is shaped to spell out "Austin"—you'll find a traditional Japanese teahouse. Inside, you'll find a plaque affixed to the wall with Isamu's essay "Spirit of the Garden" emblazoned on it. In the short essay, Taniguchi explains his reasoning for the undertaking and his hope in creating the garden. He writes:

It is my wish that through the construction of this visible garden, I might provide a symbol of universal peace. By observing the genuine peaceful nature of the garden, I believe we should be able to knock on the door of our conscience, which once was obliged to be the slave of the animal nature in man rather than of the humanity which resides on the other side of his heart. It is my desire for the peace of mankind which has endowed this man of old age the physical health and stamina to pile stone upon stone without a day's absence from the work for the last 18 months. It is my desire for peace of mankind which encouraged me in my voluntary labor to complete this long-dreamed gift for the City of Austin—this Oriental Garden. It is my wish that you have pleasant communion with the spirit of the garden.

So, enjoy all of Zilker Park, but be sure to make your way to the Zilker Botanical Garden, and while you're there, take some extra time to commune with the spirit of Old Man Taniguchi's garden.

AUDITORIUM SHORES

900 West Riverside Drive

Sitting along the shores of Lady Bird Lake, just west of Zilker Park, is Austin's most popular place for an outdoor concert. Though Zilker Park is the host to some of the largest festivals in America, like ACL Fest, the park that's home to Austin's largest off-leash dog park also hosts the most outdoor events and concerts of all kinds. That would be the 48.58 acres of Auditorium Shores Municipal Park, with its unbeatable views of the downtown skyline.

Beloved Austinite and blues legend Stevie Ray Vaughan loved to play at this site, and when he died in a tragic helicopter crash while at the height of his career at the age of thirty-five, there was a call for a memorial to be erected in his honor.

Standing nearly eight feet tall and perched atop a limestone base, the Stevie Ray Vaughan memorial, a bronze statue, was created by Ralph Hemick and placed here with a dedication ceremony in 1994. While viewing the statue, you might notice that Stevie isn't playing his guitar. Instead, he holds it next to him as he stands "meditatively" upright, staring out from beneath his signature wide-brim hat. Though Stevie isn't playing in the statue's main

In the Stevie Ray Vaughan Memorial Statue at Auditorium Shores, Austin's lost bluesman is commemorated at his favorite place to play for his city.

form, the sculpture also has the metal form of a shadow being permanently cast behind him, and in that shadow, he plays on forever.

Now, this lake, being a river at heart, can and will flood occasionally, but if you're at all worried for Stevie, don't fret. Any time there's even a chance of rising water, a concerned citizen always comes to put a life preserver on the statue, just to be safe.

THE '04

South of downtown, and bordering the parks, we find an important Austin neighborhood. It stretches from Interstate Highway I-35 on the east to MoPac/Loop 1 on the west. Its northern border is Lady Bird Lake, and its southern boundary is Highway 290, or Highway 71, or if that's not enough names for one place, locally we call the same road Ben White Boulevard. The postal zip code for the neighborhood is 78704, and since we're great at naming things, we just call it the '04. By the way, that's pronounced "Oh-Four," just so you know.

The neighborhood is full of cute, little and these days quite pricey bungalow houses. Many of Austin's favorite haunts, and some of its most famous residents, call this neighborhood home. Yoga studios, eclectic shops, fantastic restaurants, random street art, stone castles, hidden patisseries, packed parks, all manner of selfie stops and a plethora of authentic Austin experiences can be found right here in the '04.

This funny little neighborhood is often at the heart of Austin's weird and wonderful cultural movements. What made it play such a significant role in the city for so many decades? The short answer is that for a very long time, the living was easy, and the rent was cheap. So cheap, in fact, that musicians, artists and creatives of all stripes could get away with paying rent from the money they earned off their crafts or gigs, or at the very least, they often only needed to work part time to make ends meet. That economic incentive on top of the existing cultural draw meant the area became sort of a magnet for the creatives of Texas who have been moving to Austin by the VW van–full since the early 1970s, which was Austin's first modern heyday. Despite the discounted price of South Austin living for so many decades, the quality of life has always been pretty great in these parts. The parks, Lady Bird Lake, SoCo district with its many wonderful restaurants and wallet-opening shops—nearly all of it is within biking or strolling distance from just about anywhere in this neighborhood. It's also notable that the area has continued to foster its famed bohemian, artistic vibe for the most part, despite the changing demographics and rising prices. Perhaps that relaxed, creative, South Austin aura remains because of the "Keep Austin Weird" mythos, or maybe it's the sheer number of entrenched creatives who have yet to sell their bungalows to the growing tech sector crowd. Whatever the reason, we're all glad that the '04 still reigns supreme as the epicenter of the weird and wonderful South Austin scene.

PENN FIELD STATION

3601 South Congress Avenue
A few miles south of downtown on South Congress Avenue, just a bit north of Ben White Boulevard, is a water tower that rises over what is now a posh

Old airplane wings and water tower at modern Penn Field Station commemorate its historical past.

office complex but once was one of America's earliest military airfields. It carries with it a story that has connections not just to World War I but also to the Mexican Revolution, the notorious Pancho Villa himself and even the invention of the panoramic photo.

We'll begin our story in 1910 with the Mexican Revolution and its folk hero, Pancho Villa. Pancho was a living legend who killed for the first time at the age of sixteen. He was protecting the virtue of his twelve-year-old sister, who was about to become the sexual prey of a rich landowner. After killing the man, Pancho took off for the mountains, where he joined, and eventually led, the rebels who would soon start a revolution.

The United States was understandably wary of the destabilization along the border as a result of the Mexican civil war, and it wanted to have a hand in the outcome. The United States backed an ally of Pancho Villa, President Carrenza. Meanwhile, hedging its bets outside diplomacy, the U.S. Army saw an opportunity to utilize its latest, greatest, most cutting-edge military weapon: the biplane. The idea was to use the fledgling fleet as scouts and realize their potential for intelligence gathering. This brings us squarely to the invention of the panoramic photo, a resulting technology from this reconnaissance effort.

At the Pentagon, all eyes were on Mexico in 1913, and Europe was a far-off and forgotten land. North America had problems of its own. With the civil war to the south raging, a U.S. Army brigadier general testified before Congress that San Antonio was the single most strategic location in the whole of the southern United States. By 1914, the rumblings in Europe had grown, and the Great War was beginning to ignite. When it rains it pours, and at nearly the same time that war was exploding in Europe, the U.S.-backed president of Mexico mentioned earlier had a falling out with Pancho Villa. With the U.S. Army supporting Carrenza, Villa came to see America as his enemy. In 1916, Villa gathered more than one thousand men, taking them over the border on a raid of Columbus, New Mexico. This was the first foreign attack on American soil since the War of 1812, when the British sacked and burned the White House. Add to this volatile cocktail the "Zimmerman Telegram," an intercepted missive between Germany and the Mexican government. The telegram suggested an alliance between the two nations in opposition to the United States and would have been a recipe for a potential U.S. disaster on two fronts.

With the fight in Europe growing, the specific threat from Pancho Villa's rebel armies and now the greater threat from Mexico in general, a new sense of urgency took hold for the growth of a formidable airborne military force and a base to house it. The present home of the U.S. Army Air Corps, Fort Sam Houston in San Antonio, was simply too small to grow the aviation program, so a new base was created just down the road at Kelly Airfield. The base has grown over the decades and is now Kelly Air Force Base for the U.S. Air Force.

By 1917, years of fighting had been endured by soldiers and citizens all around the globe. In response to the urgent need to keep up with their

Curtiss JN-4D Biplanes awaiting flight at Penn Field, 1918. *Air Service, United States Army.*

enemies' technological advantage, America had committed to grow its cadre of capable pilots, and the site of operations in San Antonio was set for major expansion. Common sense dictates that all of these cadets would need a place to fly to and safely land, as well as repair and refuel their fragile planes during training. That's when city leaders in Austin sniffed an opportunity to join the burgeoning world of aviation. Fortuitously, at the very same moment the city of Austin was trying to position itself to be a landing field and training location, the University of Texas at Austin was interested in teaching aviation and radio science courses. The two entities worked together to select a plot of land to offer to the U.S. Army Corps of Engineers for that purpose.

By early 1918, approval had been granted for the construction of the new School of Military Aeronautics at Penn Field. It would be equipped with a radio operators' school, a landing field and support services for the Kelly Airfield students to use.

November 1918 saw the first hints of a much-wished-for cessation of fighting when an armistice was signed. With the need for a large air corps now waning, Penn Field finished training its final recruits. A few months later, the great powers of the world signed the Treaty of Versailles, ushering in an all too brief era of peace and ending the Great War once and for all. By 1919, the school and its airfield were officially shuttered, and the site was auctioned off for pennies on the dollar.

The aerial scouts never found Pancho Villa, by the way. No, the biplanes of the time weren't up to the harshness of desert flight, and they were even worse in the mountains. It turns out that those were the two places they might have spotted him. As a matter of fact, no one ever caught Pancho at all. Eventually, the Mexican government pleaded with him to retire as a rebel leader and stop raising armies against them. He agreed to hang up his gun and disband his forces in exchange for immunity and a hacienda in one of his favorite places where he could enjoy his golden years.

ST. EDWARD'S UNIVERSITY

3001 South Congress Avenue
When folks look at the history of St. Edward's University and see that the esteemed founder of the vaunted Notre Dame University in Indiana is also the founder of this fine institution, they might get a bit starstruck. If a person stopped at that low-hanging fruit, they'd get a nibble, but they'd also miss the

Intricate stonework of St. Edward's University's Main Building.

true prize, which is the story of the woman who donated the land in the first place, one Mary Doyle.

By the time the donation was made, Mary, a devout Catholic, was widowed. Since the loss of her husband, she had taken on stewardship of the family's many holdings. Luckily for her heirs and for history, Mary Doyle had noble plans for how to bequeath the many assets she and her husband had accumulated in their successful lives as one of Texas' and Austin's founding families.

Mary's husband, James, was born in Ireland sometime around 1795. By 1835, he and Mary were answering the call to settle what was then the Mexican territory of Texas. They took on a league of land (around 4,400 acres) in western Bastrop County. Who knows? Perhaps it was the smoke from their home fires that drove Uncle Billy Barton to move up the river to Waterloo. Either way, they were right behind him, and by the 1840s, the family had moved to the new capital city and taken up full-time residence in Austin.

James was a stonemason by trade. His talents were in demand in this young town, and by 1853, two big things happened for the Doyle family. First, Mr. Doyle was named superintendent of construction on the first stone capital building of Texas. James, with the labor of his slaves, successfully took on the construction project, and that windfall of a job allowed the second big thing to happen for the Doyle family: the purchase of 498 acres of land just south of Austin, which would become the Doyle family farm. From immigrant to pioneer settler to founding father, James Doyle truly lived the Texan, if not the American, dream.

Slavery can be a surprisingly complicated topic in the history of the South, especially in Austin. It can be hard to square the good deeds done by seemingly decent people with the reality of their engagement in the practice of human trafficking and slavery. Still, without any merit being given to the practice, it can be said that not all slave owners were alike. Some engaged in this inhumane practice differently than others. This is supported not only in the historical record concerning Mary and James Doyle, who in both life and death were known to treat the enslaved people in their family with a higher level of dignity than you might expect, but it's also clear from the modern-day reunions that include families of both races coming together to celebrate their ties to Mary Doyle and, most importantly, their ties to one another. "These were decent people, these Irish Catholics who were involved in slavery. They chose a compassionate route to slavery, and it's evidenced by the continued relationships after slavery," said Joseph Collins, Doyle family historian.

Emancipation in Texas didn't happen as soon as for the rest of the nation. Due to its far-flung location, freedom didn't come to people of color here until June 19, 1865. This is the root of the holiday celebrated around the country known as Juneteenth. Just months after the Civil War ended and emancipation finally arrived in Austin, James Doyle died. This left Mary to run the family business and decide the manner in which the dozen or so people they had previously kept as slaves would be treated under this new social contract. These people weren't just servants to Mary, and by all accounts it's said that she saw them as people and even as her kin.

With her remaining years, Mary used her business acumen to grow the family's holdings and secure their financial future. With her immediate family set, she turned her attention outward. In her last will and testament, she left more than 1,700 acres near Bastrop to the freed men and women who still worked with her farms. These plots of land became the foundation for one of America's early freedmen's colonies, known as St. Mary's Colony. After Mary parceled out all the land, she meticulously set aside specific items in her will to be left to those she knew could use them the most. Items like milk cows, teams of oxen or farm equipment would go to the people she'd had lifelong friendships with. Her hope was that they could use these things after her death to secure a new future for themselves and their families. In 1979, at the age of ninety-nine, one former St. Mary's resident, Benjamine Thompson, told the *Austin American-Statesman*, "A lot of whites held us as slaves and turned us loose with nothing, Old lady Doyle didn't do that. She gave that land to her colored slaves, and their ancestors grew up to have families."

It was likely during this larger moment in her life, this moment of pondering what positive impact she could leave on the world after her death, that Mary decided to donate the Austin farm to the Catholic Church. This is where we get to our famous founder, Reverend Edward Sorin. The school isn't named after him, by the way; it's actually named for his patron saint, St. Edward the Confessor and King.

Reverend Sorin of the Holy Cross Fathers and Brothers came to America as a missionary, fresh from seminary in France, with six other clergymen in 1840. Soon after, he was hard at work laying the foundations for what would eventually become Notre Dame University near South Bend, Indiana. His life's work, the university, was built, burned and built again—this time bigger and better and considered a monument to

Angels in the alcoves hidden on the campus of St. Edward's University.

Catholicism itself. His order gained in size and influence over the decades that followed his arrival, and by the early 1870s, the order was helping to staff a newly established Catholic college in Galveston. That's where word got to Reverend Sorin that a widow in Austin had a dream of building a college, and rather notably, she not only had the land to build it on but was also eager to gift that land to the church. After speaking with Mary in 1872, an agreement was reached. Sorin accepted the tract of land, and Mary passed away soon after in early 1873. While in Austin, Sorin was also able to secure a second, adjacent tract of 123 acres for the college, which was donated by Willis L. Robards.

Unable to begin construction immediately, yet wisely unwilling to let the resource go to waste, Sorin sent two young Brothers of the Cross down to Austin to begin working the farmland in 1874. By 1881, with the first students trickling in, two modest wood structures had been built, and by 1885, the school had been chartered by the State of Texas as St. Edward's College. In 1889, famed Austin architect Nicholas J. Clayton built the first main building. That building burned down in 1903, as was the theme with Reverend Sorin, and the same architect came back for a second go at it.

In 1917, the school donated some of its land to Austin's Penn Field venture, and the same 1922 tornado that tore through the repurposed airfield also struck a dorm at St. Edward's University. Sadly, one student was killed in this act of God.

By 1925, the college had grown into a full-fledged university charter, and today, St. Edward's University educates nearly five thousand students each year in a variety of highly regarded liberal arts undergraduate programs, as well as many highly competitive graduate programs. The university operates under an endowment in excess of $100 million. Such grand growth from a widow's simple dream.

To get the most out of your visit, use the university's website to arrange a tour. There's much to learn about the history of the school, and if you can avoid getting too starstruck by the big names, you might just find some quiet folks who made some big waves.

SOCO DISTRICT

If Austin has a main street, it's Congress Avenue. The street lies almost dead center of town and stretches in practically razor-straight fashion for nearly half the length of the city. This single thoroughfare connects the University

Historic SoCo shopping and entertainment district.

of Texas, the new Texas State Mall, the Bob Bullock Texas History Museum, the Texas State Capitol, downtown Austin, Lady Bird Lake, the Texas School for the Deaf, SoCo shopping district, the '04 neighborhood, St. Edward's University and then it still goes on and on.

One must-experience section of this street stretches for just over a mile, from Lady Bird Lake to Oltorf Street, and is chockfull of all manner of fun. Nearly everyone who visits Austin gets the recommendation to stroll "SoCo" for the shopping, food and famous music venues, but in historical truth, things haven't always been that way. For the first one hundred years of life in Austin, anything south of Lady Bird Lake was farmland. The first semi-reliable version of a road on this side of the Colorado River was a dirt lane built in the 1850s, and that was just fine for the needs of the locals all the way up to the turn of the twentieth century. In 1910, the road was laid over with bricks, and tracks were set for trolley cars that would clang up and down Congress through the 1940s. It would be during that four-decade stretch that the very first shops began sprouting up just south of the Texas School for the Deaf. As the 1950s came around, automobiles increased in use, and Congress Avenue was the first paved road in town. It was in this era that the oldest buildings were mostly torn down, and we would see the construction of the shops and buildings that would continue to shape the architectural aesthetic that we find in modern-day SoCo. Today, we see a new round of multi-use development along this historic route, ensuring the continued relevance of this district for years to come.

TEXAS SCHOOL FOR THE DEAF

1102 South Congress Avenue
The Texas School for the Deaf is situated between South Congress Avenue and South 1ˢᵗ Street. The 67.5-acre campus provides safe housing for nearly half its students, as well as educational and vocational opportunities for the children of Texas who have been born with deafness and other similar physical challenges.

The school owes its very existence to nothing less than good timing. Back in 1856, the Sixth Legislative Session was underway in Austin while Elisha Pease was governor. Pease, whom we met earlier in our adventure, is considered to be the father of Texas public education for his part in creating the financial system that would fund schools around the state. At the same time, that the Sixth Session was underway, Austin had a visitor. The stranger from the north was a deaf man by the name of Matthew Clark. Clark had the opportunity to ask the legislation if Texas had a school dedicated to the hearing impaired. The answer was no, but that's a fine idea, and we'll get right on it. Governor Pease immediately set about the task of appointing a commission to get a school for the deaf up and running as quickly as possible.

Clark was appointed to travel around the surrounding counties to see if there were in fact any deaf children in need of an education. If any deaf children were located, it would also fall upon Clark to convince their parents to allow the children to be educated away from home, sending them instead to the new school in Austin. It turns out that four boys who fit the bill were found in that first search, and the school opened its doors on January 2, 1857.

One of the reasons that the school is able to claim the title of "longest continually operational public school in Texas" dates back to that moment of the school's creation. It was also during that legislative session that "an act setting aside and appropriating land for the benefit of asylums" passed both the Texas House and Senate, and 100,000 acres of land was allocated for sale and lease to sustain this and other similar social institutions around the state. In the years that followed, the amount of land available to support the asylum school systems grew to include more than 410,000 acres. These large plots had been set aside for Indigenous people of Texas, but the last of these Native families had been forcibly removed from the state by 1859, and their land was added to the rest of the acreage that was available to be sold in support of the asylums.

The school has seen good times and bad over its many years of operation. During the American Civil War, no salaries were paid, yet these dedicated

Texas School for the Deaf, the longest-running public school in Texas.

teachers and their many students remained. With little support coming in, they had to fend for themselves by growing their own food and making their clothes from wool gathered off sheep they raised on site.

The school now cares for the needs of more than 550 students ranging from eighteen months to seventeen years of age and provides support services to more than 7,000 additional students statewide. Its 450 teachers and staff operate off a budget that in 2014 was just under $28 million. To say that this tenacious school has come a long way from its humble beginnings is indisputable.

If you're on the South 1st Street side of the school and have ever watched the television series *Friday Night Lights* that aired from 2006 to 2011, you might recognize the sprawling athletic areas and football field. The iconic campus was used as one of the many local backdrops for the series and driving by is always a favorite for fans of the show.

THE ANN RICHARDS MEMORIAL BRIDGE (BAT BRIDGE)

Congress Avenue crossing Lady Bird Lake

This historic bridge is named in honor of Ann Richards. She was the forty-fifth governor of Texas, the second woman to hold the office, and she served from 1991 to 1995. Governor Richards came to national attention with her keynote address to the 1988 Democratic National Convention. Known for her wit and humor, she didn't disappoint when she finally got the spotlight, saying that George Bush Sr., the GOP nominee for president, was "born with a silver foot in his mouth." The joke landed, and she spent some time as the subject of talk around water coolers and as an inspiration to comedians across America.

As governor, she was a loud and frequent proponent of Austin and its cultural significance as "the live music capital of the world." It was often mentioned when she spoke with the press or gave speeches, such as another keynote address, this one given to the SXSW Conference in 1993. It should be noted that any rumors that she coined the "live music capital" phrase are purely apocryphal, though she did help make the nickname stick. Governor Richards was a larger-than-life woman, and she made a big impact on Austin that endures long after her death. One way that Austin has chosen to remember her legacy was by naming our main street's bridge after her when she passed away in 2006.

This bridge connects Congress Avenue downtown to South Congress Avenue by spanning its concrete arches over Lady Bird Lake. Every year from spring to fall, you can see hundreds of people lining up on top of the east side of the bridge, all of them jockeying for the best spot to bear witness to a natural spectacle. These folks are hoping to catch a glimpse of Austin's most beloved of critters, the Mexican free-tail bats. In truth, those on top of the bridge are in the worst spot to see the bats, but that's why you've got this book.

First, some historical perspective. Lady Bird Lake, as we've noted, is in fact a dammed-up section of the Lower Colorado River. The river was tamed long ago by the dam builders of the 1960s who, with the backing of LBJ, created the Highland Lakes of the Texas Hill Country to service power generation plants and bring electrification to the far reaches of rural central Texas.

For the first twenty years as a settlement on the edge of the Texas frontier, as both Waterloo and as Austin, the only way to cross the river was to get wet. If the water was low enough, you'd be fine, but if it was too

An 1889 Austin map in relief and cast in metal, located at the northwest foot of the Congress Bridge.

high you might be out of luck if you and your horse weren't both strong swimmers, and you could just forget about your wagons. It wasn't until the 1840s that a ferry was available to aid in crossing in exchange for a toll. The ferry held its monopoly on transit all the way to 1852. That's when a pontoon bridge was erected, also with a toll for crossing. The pontoon bridge held up until 1869, so its builders surely made their investment back and then some. That was followed in 1875, during Reconstruction from the Civil War, with the first wooden bridge over the river. Between the bridge and related dyke work, the price tag came in at around $100,0000 for the build, a pretty penny at the time. It turns out the wooden bridge would last less than ten years, and in 1884, a "modern" iron bridge was erected with private money and then purchased later by the City of Austin just in time to expand outside the once geographically locked city limits.

All that growth in the early 1900s that we mentioned while discussing SoCo led the city to rebuild the bridge again in 1908. This time coming in at a cost of almost $210,000, the arched concrete form that we see today first took shape and opened to the public in 1910.

The final chapter of the bridge's construction history is the selfsame chapter that brings us back to the bats. The year was 1980, and the bridge required major renovations. The design for the reconstruction called for the new road to basically sit atop several rather large concrete boxes, and those boxes in turn rest over the original concrete arches. There's a space between the concrete boxes that allows for the swelling and shrinking the material naturally experiences during our dramatic temperature changes. Though simply being a functional artifact of the design, that man-made crevice is like a dream house for the Mexican free-tail bat. Before the change in design, there wasn't a place beneath the bridge for these bats to live, and after its construction, as many bats as could fit moved in, which in this case was 750,000 pregnant mother bats, each with 1 pup, or 1,500,000 bats. It's worth noting at this point that their sudden and unexpected appearance downtown brought with them a somewhat understandable touch of anti-bat hysteria to Austin at the time.

Despite our brief hysteria, bats, as a species, are pretty amazing by almost any standard. Let's start by harkening back to biology class to recall that bats are indeed mammals that have somehow evolved to include flight into their bag of tricks, but flight is hardly their only superpower. For example, we mentioned that the bats beneath the bridge are all mothers and pups. (Populations of bats are separated by sex into male and female colonies.) When the time finally comes, those mothers are able to control gestation in some astounding ways that make scientists take note. A pregnant bat can not only choose when to give birth, which in itself is incredible, but that moment she chooses is always in synchronicity with the other mothers. When these gals do give birth, it's to a pup that's up to a third of its mother's size—an enormous baby by any standard! Why all of these incredible specializations in regard to how and when they give birth? What could push a mammal down such an extreme evolutionary path? It has everything to do with why all of those people on top of the bridge are in the wrong spot and might leave disappointed from not seeing very many bats from above. The reason is simple: these bats may be monster predators to insects, but to several native predatory birds that fly in the sky and to many of the large, hungry fish that swim beneath the bridge, these bats are an easy snack. As such, they go to great lengths to stay alive, such as evolving some extraordinary biological traits or simply hiding beneath the bridge until it's dark enough to make a break for it.

At the height of the Austin bat season, when all the moms and pups are out hunting, the colony will devour more than thirty thousand pounds of insects, mostly mosquitoes, each night. For a way to frame that number in your mind, that's around the same weight as nineteen cows, so we could call it a herd's worth of mosquitoes eaten by the bats each night. Clearly these bats are doing us a major service, but that wasn't immediately apparent when the colony first showed up. A few small but vocal bat-eradication groups sprang up as a response from concerned citizens. Those folks simply hadn't had a chance to speak to Merlin Tuttle. Dr. Tuttle quit his job as the curator of mammals (specializing in, you guessed it, bats) at the Milwaukee Museum. The reason for his resignation was the noble pursuit of his passion, and the founding of Bat Conservation International, or BCI. Dr. Tuttle chose to relocate to Austin to start BCI because it was the largest city in America stricken with bat hysteria at the time, and he was out to change hearts and minds in favor of protecting and coexisting with these special creatures. It took time and patience, but the efforts of Dr. Tuttle and BCI were not in vain, and eventually he succeeded in turning the tide of public opinion. Today, Austin embraces our winged neighbors, and we've even erected the Night Wing Bat sculpture at the southwest foot of the bridge. It's been estimated that revenue generated by bat tourism tops $10 million annually in Austin, so it's safe to assume they'll be welcome here for a long time to come.

When you visit the bats, here's your insider's tip. First, knowingly walk past all the folks on the bridge until you come to a staircase on the southeast side. Take the stairs down to ground level and walk a few feet north and

Curious onlookers from above and below as a cloud of bats emerges from beneath the Congress bridge at sunset.

toward the lake. You'll notice a wide-open space between the bridge and the tree line; this is the bat viewing area. From below the bridge, on land or by boat, you'll get the very best view of the show, and it really is quite a show. When a group of bats is roosted in their home, it's known as a colony, but when a group of bats takes flight it takes on a new name and becomes a "cloud" of bats. This cloud is so big that at sunset, its resulting "bio scatter" can clearly be seen like a thunderstorm suddenly erupting on Doppler radar screens across central Texas. The colony below the Ann Richards Bridge claims the honor of being the largest urban bat colony on earth, and if you get a good spot to watch their departure, you'll surely agree it's a sight. Just take this advice, and don't look up in awe, mouth agape with wonder, for too long. They've been holed up all day, after all.

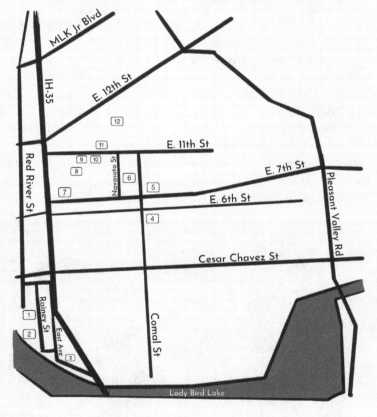

EAST AUSTIN

1. RAINEY STREET DISTRICT
2. MACC
3. EAST AVENUE
4. EAST 6TH STREET
5. HUSTON-TILLOTSON UNIV
6. TEXAS STATE CEMETERY
7. FRENCH LEGATION
8. EBENEZER BAPTIST CHURCH
9. TEXAS MUSIC HISTORY MUSEUM
10. RHAPSODY MOSAIC
11. VICTORY GRILL
12. GEORGE WASHINGTON CARVER MUSEUM

RAINEY STREET HISTORIC DISTRICT

To the longtime Austinite, Rainey Street surely seemed an unlikely place to suddenly sprout dozens of bars and become one of the busiest nightlife scenes in the American South. After all, it was forever nothing more than a few quiet blocks of old bungalow houses that had seen their glory days come and go. Once upon a time, it was a thriving upper-middle-class neighborhood mostly housing the families of skilled laborers. A major flood in 1935 stopped any future would-be home builders in their tracks, and the construction of I-35 Highway, in 1956, geographically isolated these homes from the rest of their neighbors. Strictly speaking, Rainey Street District is located downtown, but its heart lies with its neighbors on the other side of the highway, so we're taking a liberty and returning this neighborhood to its roots as part of the neighborhood we now call "East Austin." This isolation caused by the location of the highway further dampened the prospects of any revitalization of the area and, in the process, inadvertently created a bit of a time capsule in the form of these historic structures that survived into the modern era.

This small cluster of modest homes was originally the brainchild of Frank Rainey and famed cattleman/would-be hotelier Jesse Driskill. The two business partners bought the 120-acre plot between Water Street and

Dozens of restaurants, bars and food trucks line the Rainey Street Historic District.

the Colorado River in 1884, and the houses were built and rebuilt from 1885 to 1935, which, again, was when that big flood destroyed or damaged much of the area.

In 1985, a group of local preservationists succeeded in getting the neighborhood listed in the National Register of Historic Places and provided the district with some level of protection against the encroaching construction downtown. By 2004, the city had rezoned the area to permit commercial development with a process that incentivized maintaining the historic aesthetic of this neighborhood, while still encouraging a change in the use of these structures and lots from residential to commercial.

Today, this once quiet street is anything but, as each night it packs the visitors, locals, bachelorette partiers and conventioneers into the dozens of bars, restaurants and food trucks filling up every site on the street. No matter which spot you spend the most time in, Rainey Street is always a party and always a great place to make some friends and hear lots of Austin's legendary live music.

EMMA S. BARRIENTOS MEXICAN AMERICAN CULTURAL CENTER

600 River Street

Nearly halfway down Rainey Street lies the entrance to the Emma S. Barrientos Mexican American Cultural Center. The MACC is an architectural gem with its semicircular white form and sprawling green plaza. It's also the fruit of an effort that began decades before the well-attended groundbreaking ceremony in late 2007.

The MACC was the brainchild of the leaders of Austin's Chicano Movement in the 1970s. These politicians, teachers, artists, educators and citizens recognized a need for a space that would be "dedicated to the preservation, creation, presentation, and promotion of Mexican American cultural arts and heritage." Over a span of forty years, the grassroots effort behind this center would have to overcome obstacles, navigate the city's labyrinthine processes, work with the task forces and carve out the feasibility studies. After decades of concerted effort, the group finally pulled out its first win in the late 1980s when it was able to secure this site for its needs. The warehouse that sat onsite, however, was not up to the task of realizing this shared community vision. There was yet more to do, so the grassroots effort would continue organizing, fundraising and working with the city to find ways to create a bond to

A view of the architecture of the Emma S. Barrientos Mexican American Cultural Center.

cover the expected construction costs for the thirty-thousand-square-foot site and its twenty-two-thousand-square-foot plaza.

The project has been divided into three phases, and the first phase is what we see at the time of this book's writing. Phases two and three are being finalized after a period of public input that was collected in 2018. The estimated cost for full construction comes in at around $50 million. As it stands, phase one provides a theater, performance spaces, art galleries, classrooms and office space. That's in addition to the Lady Bird Lake–facing plaza that's always open to passersby needing a break from the hike and bike trail. With its stunning architectural form and landscaping features on the outside and its year-round programming utilizing the creative and educational spaces bringing in more than fifty thousand people a year inside, the MACC is surpassing all expectations as it continues to serve our entire community with its spotlight on Latino culture and heritage.

EAST AVENUE

The original layout of Austin had East Avenue as the eastern border, and as the city grew beyond the original grid, that street became the gateway to the communities that, for a time, came to thrive there. Specifically, these neighborhoods became the home to Austin's Latino community and our Black community, and this was in no way by accident.

In 1928, looking to solve the problems of any growing city, like how to pay for schools and sidewalks and meet the growing need for water and power, the city council brought in an outside consulting agency to create a "Master Plan." This would be the first comprehensive plan for growth ever made by the city leadership. Since this was the Jim Crow era, one of the problems these leaders felt the need to grapple with was how to maintain the grip of segregation in a city with thriving mixed racial areas all over town, while avoiding the expensive duplication of parks, schools and bus stops. Instead of abandoning segregation entirely or allowing mixed racial neighborhoods to remain but separating the entrances to buildings or having separate water fountains for white and Black residents, the city would instead just work to fully segregate the entire town's population into strict racial and geographical districts. This would prove to be a decision that would reverberate with consequence even up to this day.

The East Austin area was originally owned by the French Legation before being sold to a local family. In the years following the American Civil War and emancipation, this family sold plots to former slaves,

A street sign framed by new construction is the last remnant of once bustling East Avenue.

creating in the area a bustling freedmen's colony just outside the city. This wasn't the only freedmen's neighborhood around town, however. We already saw Clarksville on the far west side of 6th Street; another, called Wheatsville, was just north of UT Austin; and there were several more around the outskirts of town as well.

In regard to the segregation challenge, the consultants were frank in their findings, reporting, "In our studies in Austin we have found that the negroes [*sic*] are present in small numbers, in practically all sections of the city, excepting the area just east of East Avenue and south of the City Cemetery. This area seems to be all negro population." They continued with their answer to the issue: "It is our recommendation that the nearest approach to the solution of the race segregation problem will be the recommendation of this district as a negro district; and that all the facilities and conveniences be provided the negroes in this district as an incentive to draw the negro population to this area. This will eliminate the necessity of duplication of white and black schools, white and black parks, and other duplicate facilities for this area." Perhaps to assuage any pesky tinges of guilt, they added, "We further recommend that the negro schools in this area be provided with ample and adequate playground space and facilities similar to the white schools of the city."

The city council unanimously adopted the plan and called for the relocation of communities of color to the area we now call East Austin. For a Black family to defy the rezoning and stay in their homes was to endure years of neglect and harassment by the city. With the rare exception of a few holdouts such as the longtime homeowners in Clarksville, the city became fully segregated in short order. No longer allowing multiracial neighborhoods meant Austin's racial groups would progress for decades with an unusually high degree of isolation from one another.

Latino communities at the time were in relatively small numbers in Austin, and since they didn't seem to pose a direct threat to the establishment, they weren't subjected to the same systemic levels of racial barriers until their numbers began growing. By this point, at a time when overt race laws were beginning to lose more and more court challenges, the powers that be shifted to utilizing the tactic of redlining that had been so successful with maintaining the racial barriers with the Black communities. As a result, the small print of Austin's social contract would change from "No Blacks" to read "Whites Only," therefore increasing the range of this racial weapon and keeping loans and services out of the reach of the growing populations of any people of color.

The creation of Highway I-35 in 1956, atop what was East Avenue, put a physical barrier where a cultural and legal barrier had long sat. In some ways, that separation also created a somewhat safer space for the people of color who lived there. A Black resident of the time, Eva Lindsey, was once quoted as saying, "It's like they dropped us off here and forgot about us." The East Side became a place where these men and women could raise families and build churches, schools, fraternal organizations and businesses that were accessible to other people of color like themselves, so long as they didn't venture into that other, white Austin. This, at a time when both the empowered Caucasian culture and legal system were openly systematically hostile to anyone classified as non-white.

Over the decades, local laws changed, but segregation was engrained so deeply in the community that many of the neighborhood's families remained fixed in place. From Lady Bird Lake to around 7th Street, you would mostly find Hispanic families, and from 8th Street to MLK Jr. Boulevard, you would mostly find the Black community, with its center being East 11th Street.

Time, plus the lack of access to capital, eventually took its toll on many of the buildings on the East Side. With the homes increasingly falling into the fixer-upper category, the neighborhood, with its deep potential for development and incredible location, was ripe for gentrification. By the early 2000s, at the beginning of Austin's extended tech and real estate boom, these once ignored plots and increasingly dilapidated structures started rising steadily in value to relatively astronomical sums. As this new wave of Austin immigrants rushed to buy a piece of town to call their own, the East Side was one of the first areas to be bought up. By the 2010s, the demographics had firmly changed to include more and more of the high-earning technology workers who were relocating to Austin in droves. With racial segregation abolished in the courts long ago, suddenly the only color that seemed to matter was green, and if you plan to buy your own little slice of the East Side, you'd better have lots of it these days. Still, despite all the changes, a new community is forming in the neighborhood, and it's a mix of these generational families and the new Austin that we explore today.

EAST 6TH STREET

The East 6th Street District is home to some of Austin's oldest and newest watering holes and eateries. A full exploration of the area is highly recommended to those who like to indulge their senses, and if you really want to experience it in its glory, an evening visit is the time to go. That's when, on any given night of the week, thousands of Austinites and tourists alike fill the many restaurants, food trucks, music venues, bars, breweries and dance halls that stretch for blocks and blocks on end.

It's true that 6th Street can be a tad confusing for a visitor because there's actually four very different and distinct entertainment districts on this one street. Each one has a nickname or two that the locals use to identify the various parts of town. This section is simply called East 6th to most locals, and the section that is just west of I-35 is the more famous Dirty 6th section that most visitors have heard of. It's bewildering because if you're standing on Dirty 6th and look at the street signs, they also say East 6th, but the differences are palpable. There's also the West 6th District between Congress and Lamar, and from Lamar to MoPac Highway, we have Clarksville, the former freedmen's colony near the Treaty Oak that now offers amazing restaurants, bars and art galleries. We'll visit Dirty 6th and West 6th later in the adventure.

Murals line the buildings along East 6th Street Entertainment District.

HUSTON-TILLOTSON UNIVERSITY

900 Chicon Street

One block farther north of the bar district, Bluebonnet Hill rises overhead, and sitting atop is the campus of Huston-Tillotson University. As the hyphenated name suggests, this traditional Black college was born of two separate intuitions that came together to better serve their similar missions and mandates.

Tracing its roots all the way back to 1875, as the first seat of higher education in Austin, Tillotson Collegiate and Normal Institute, as it was originally called, was built by the Freedmen's Aid Society. For those not familiar with the term, a "normal institute" was a college that taught educators, and this one specifically was set up to train and educate African Americans in a post-emancipation world. Due to their circumstances, many of the one hundred students who attended the inaugural year had never received any formal education before arriving at the campus. There was an understanding among these gentlemen that education was a privilege that came with the burden of enriching their community. The students were eager to learn, and many excelled in their scholastic ambitions. Over the years, the school grew, and the name changed slightly, as did its focus, from time to time. In 1925, it was reorganized as a community college, but by the next year, it had a different vision and became a successful women's college. This version of the school lasted until it became a co-ed senior college in 1931.

Huston-Tillotson University sitting atop Bluebonnet Hill.

Huston College, on the other hand, began slightly after Tillotson, with its creation in 1876, under a different name. The Methodist minister who founded it, Reverend George Warren Richardson, came to Dallas from Minnesota with a passion and a commitment to the advancement of Black youth. The school moved to Austin just two years later in 1878, into what is now the site of Wesley Methodist Church. Like Tillotson College, this too was a normal institute, but the school also taught bookkeeping, religion and blacksmithing. The institute changed its name and configuration over the years as was needed, until 1887, when an Iowa farmer named Samuel Huston donated property worth more than $10,000 at the time, with the sole condition being that a college would bear his name. It took a while to accomplish, but in 1910, the school made the change and was chartered as Samuel Huston College, receiving its accreditation in 1934.

By the early 1950s, the two colleges enjoyed a healthy rivalry with each other, but resources in the supporting community were scarce and the missions of the two schools overlapped in such a compatible way that the decision was made by the trustees to merge the institutions. In October 1952, the same year Azie Morton would begin school, a new charter was signed as Huston-Tillotson College, and it moved into its present campus.

In 2005, the college changed its name one last time to become Huston-Tillotson University to reflect its increased resources and academic offerings. Be sure to check the website for a tour of this historic campus.

TEXAS STATE CEMETERY

909 Navasota Street
The Texas State Cemetery has become the eternal resting place for some of the greatest and the bravest among us, and it truly is an honor for a person to be allowed to occupy a space inside the grounds. The cemetery is divided into two main sections. One half holds the graves of Confederate soldiers. The other half of the cemetery holds the graves and cenotaphs of many of Texas's biggest political names, historical figures and most honored soldiers, such as the father of Texas himself, Stephen F. Austin.

As you would imagine, there are very strict rules regarding who can be buried at this cemetery, which are codified in state law. The rules basically come down to having served as any state elected official, serving as a unanimously approved appointed official with a long career or being

Lone Star flag unfurls over the Texas State Cemetery.

recommended by the governor. Even still, the last two options are subject to committee approval.

The cemetery dates back to 1851 and the death of yet another complicated Texas hero, the "Old Indian Fighter," aka Senator Edward Burleson. To speak of Burleson's life is to basically recite the most action-packed chapters of early Texas history. He was born an army brat who grew up on the battlefield with his father, an army commander named James B. Burleson. He was fighting his first battles under his father's command in the War of 1812, yet it wouldn't be long before the tables would turn, and his father would be under Edward's command in the battles for Texas independence.

Burleson was the kind of guy who could, and frequently did, raise an army to fight alongside him. He could stir men's blood, inspire their courage and rally the troops. Then, with his lifetime of experience on the battlefield, he could bring that force to bear against his enemies and provide win after win for his side.

To be a founding father also requires a person occasionally replace a rifle with a pen and a canteen with a wine glass and be involved with the politics of the day. Though he would frequently have to rush away from his political duties to wield his military prowess, Burleson was continually elected to be part of most major delegations and legislative sessions in one capacity or another during and after the formation of the Republic of Texas.

Burleson was the real deal frontiersman—a tougher-than-nails soldier and trailblazer. During his life, he seems to have been involved in just about everything notable of the era. Setting aside his storied military and political careers, he also laid out the streets of Waterloo as it grew into a small town in the years just before Edwin Waller transformed it into Austin. He founded San Marcos, a neighboring town just south of Austin. He surveyed and cleared the roads that stretched out from the edge of the frontier in Bastrop and deeper still, well into the Comanche-held lands.

As you might have guessed from his nickname, this man was a frequent fighter of the now infamous skirmishes the early settlers had with the Native population. As a result, he, just like Mirabeau Lamar, was staunchly anti-Houston, both politically and personally speaking. This was a curious stance when you consider that Burleson, again like Lamar, also served as vice president to Sam Houston. It made for tenuous coalitions, to be sure.

Sam Houston grew into such an oversized political force in his lifetime that he came to literally define both parties. Politicians came to be known as being either a "Houston man" or an "anti-Houston." The disagreement between the two camps was surely nuanced and complex, but it basically boils down to this: Houston felt the gains made in the war for independence were hard won, and the fragile new nation needed to accept austerity measures. He saw the need to work on building up and protecting what little gains the young republic had made. Houston also felt the best way to accomplish this moment of foundation building was to make peace with the neighbors. Houston supported eventual statehood with America, but in the meantime, he sought and was able to secure nearly two years of peace with Mexico. As for the populations of Native Americans who had dwelled in this land for countless generations, well, Houston's absolutely fascinating back story tells you all you need to know about his long-held admiration for the Native peoples.

Houston had several distinct chapters in his life. First, in Tennessee, he came to the attention of Andrew Jackson and became his protégé. Through his connections with that inner circle, he rose to the Tennessee governorship by the time he'd reached his mid-thirties. At the same time, he took a young wife, and all seemed perfect until a few months into the marriage when, to everyone's surprise the new couple suddenly divorced, and in a major plot twist, Sam Houston resigned as governor without explanation. Houston and his ex-wife never spoke of the matter publicly, and the mystery of what exactly happened remains unknown to history. We do know that Houston, politically humiliated and divorced, left the state and took refuge with a Native tribe that he had befriended while working with them during their relocation to Oklahoma. By all accounts, Sam was a sloppy, drunken mess at this point, but the tribe took him in at his lowest depths; gave him purpose, a community and a new wife; and returned him to his health. No longer able to see these people as savages, he felt strongly that peace and coexistence with the Native population should and could be secured.

When Houston emerged back into white society after this self-imposed exile, he slowly returned to politics and then heard the call to settle Texas, where he founded Houston, his namesake city destined for greatness. Speaking of the city of Houston, one other defining political consideration was the location of the capital city. Houston, along with any respectable "Houston man," was obviously in favor of the city that bore his name reclaiming the title and the honor of Texas capital. Houston and his supporters were vehemently against the purpose-built town of Austin serving as the capital, and his disdain for their claim ultimately led us to an episode of history called the "Archive War," which we'll explore in the pages ahead.

The "anti-Houston" camp, which Burleson and Lamar both fell firmly into, saw things very differently from Houston. To them, the only way forward for Texas was expansion, and not small, incremental growth but massive expansion won through an ultimate defeat of Mexico. They envisioned an empire that would someday stretch all the way to the Pacific Ocean and include the silver mines in what we would consider New Mexico along the way. To their way of thinking, without the Native populations to contend with, the task of expansion would be much easier. As a result of this mindset, this group was totally disinterested in coexistence with the Indigenous peoples and instead sought the full removal of those populations statewide. These Texans who had fought both the Mexican army and the Comanche raiding parties for years on end were also enraged when evidence emerged of a burgeoning alliance between the Comanche Nation and the government of Mexico. At risk from this dangerous new friendship and facing the very real possibility of renewed hostilities on all fronts, the anti-Houston men felt that safety could only be found with a defeated Mexico and an exiled Native population. As for the Archive War over the location of the capital, the anti-Houston men were clearly all in favor of Austin serving as the permanent capital for the Republic of Texas.

Openly opposed to each other, but joined in coalition, Burleson, like Lamar during his tenure as vice president to Houston, would never see

Stephen F. Austin statue seen through the unique glass and wrought-iron General Johnston memorial at the Texas State Cemetery.

eye to eye with the boss. They disagreed on nearly everything, and to add insult to injury, Houston would never let his VP do what he was truly best at while in office, which was kick butt in battle. The scene was repeated more than once. Trouble would start up somewhere in Texas, and Vice President Burleson would be on the scene raising an army in no time. Next thing he knew, Sam Houston would send down another general with orders to relieve him and take over command of the troops. Despite the safe assumption that this was an offense to the proud vice president, Burleson remained ever the obedient soldier. He always stepped down and relinquished command when asked to return to his political role.

In due course, Houston's term expired. Burleson ran for the top seat in 1844, and though he lost the race, he was hardly defeated. He was easily elected into the Senate by the end of 1845. Once there, he was promptly and unanimously voted to the position of Senate president pro tem, a powerful position in its own right and one that he held for the rest of his days. Always to be found in the center of the action, Burleson even made time to command troops and fight in the Mexican-American War for a couple of years from 1846 to 1848 before hanging up his musket and finally settling full time into political life. When the end of his days finally came, the legislators purchased this plot of land just outside town as a place to bury him and to use as the Texas State Cemetery.

FRENCH LEGATION

802 San Marcos Street

The second of the six flags over Texas is that of France, and when the Republic of Texas was born from its struggle with Mexico, it was the friendship of France that helped tip the balance in the favor of revolution. When Waterloo was first transformed into Austin and began serving as our capital, the French saw an opportunity to return to the sphere of influence in the Americas and moved quickly to set up official diplomatic relation. They sent an ambassador and began construction of their embassy, known as the French Legation. It was finished in 1841 and remains one of the oldest wood-frame structures still standing in Texas.

Monsieur Jean Pierre Isidore Alphonse de Saligny was appointed the French chargé d'affaires to the fledgling nation. That's a lot of names to keep up with by anyone's standards, so he went by Alphonse de Saligny. This must have been a tough posting for M. de Saligny, who was cut from a different cloth than most of the pioneer Texans he was sent to liaise with. Despite the harshness of frontier life, de Saligny would not sink into the mire; instead, he would bring some culture and sophistication to the muddy streets of the new capital and offer an example of civilization to its roughly hewn residents. Alas, in the end, things didn't exactly go as he planned.

When he arrived in Austin, de Saligny was forced by circumstance to take up residence at our first inn, the Bullock House, and he was hardly alone there. The hotel opened in 1839 and was located in the heart of it all, on the northwest corner of what we now consider to be 6th and Congress. Still important today, it was also the first intersection in town and mere steps away from the first capitol buildings. By choosing that location, Alphonse was also lodging alongside and rubbing elbows with many of the visiting

The historic French Legation, oldest frame structure in Austin and the site of the "Pig War."

Texas officials of the time. Combine all that with the fact that the Bullock House was the center of social life in Austin for many years, and you can get a sense that this place was hopping.

Having secured access to the movers and shakers of this new frontier nation, de Saligny had big plans for Texas and its relationship with France, so he got right to work. It should be noted as a reminder that France was a world superpower in this era, and the offer being made by de Saligny was basically access to loans with favorable terms from France, a financial lifeline to keep the government of the Texas Republic running and also much-needed military protection from a still seething Mexican army, from the raids of the Native Americans and, just in case it was ever needed, to provide a deterrent to the expanding United States. Obviously, the French would have to move in to supply that support, so Texas would be expected to allow increased settlement by French citizens in addition to the military bases de Saligny wanted to build.

Skeptical detractors of the plan were hesitant to willfully invite a major military power to establish a standing army and allow the construction of multiple permanent fortifications on Texas soil. Equally disconcerting was the proposed settlements populated solely by civilian foreign

French chargé d'affaires to the Republic of Texas Alphonse de Saligny. *Maria Chenu, engraver, from photo by Alexandre Ken, 1862.*

nationals in support of that army. To some, this would seem like a clear return of the French empire into North America via Texas. The idea was a hard sell to men still weary from their many battles for freedom with an occupying army.

Bullock Hotel

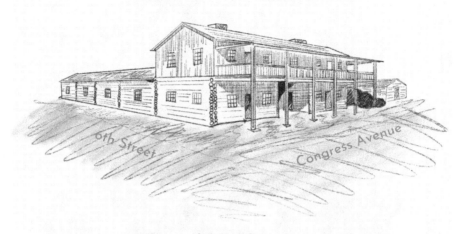

Austin, Republic of Texas - 1839

Bullock Hotel, built in 1839. It was the source of the wayward pigs that changed the fate of world politics in the "Pig War."

Despite the naysayers, de Saligny had some initial success getting a bill in support of his measure passed through the Texas House of Representatives, and around that same time, in early 1841, his workers had at long last built enough of the Legation to allow him to move out of his temporary accommodations at the Bullock House. He and his servants would finally take up full-time residence in his grand homage to France and the fine culture that it represents. Perched atop its hill, the twenty-one-acre property was larger and finer than the capitol site at the time. Things were looking up for Alphonse and for France.

Unfortunately for all involved, some hogs escaped from the Bullock plantation and followed the chargé d'affaires to his new estate. Pigs being pigs, they tore up the place. In one complaint, M. de Saligny claimed the hogs had "invaded the stables of his horses, ate their corn, and even penetrated to his very bedroom to devour his linen and chew his papers." That's not even to mention the uprooted fences and devastated decorative gardens. No longer willing to let the offenses go unchallenged, it was a death sentence for the livestock. Strict orders were given to his servant to kill any and all pig invaders on sight. Depending on who you ask, somewhere between five and twenty-five hogs lost their lives under this order.

Enraged, Bullock demanded reparations for the lost livestock. De Saligny, citing diplomatic immunity, refused to pay up. Bullock wasn't having it, and the next time he saw the ambassador's servant in town, he severely and publicly whipped the man and threatened to do the same to his master. The scene was a source of deep embarrassment to Alphonse and, by extension, an insult to France. De Saligny insisted that the Republic of Texas would have to punish Bullock if the offense would ever be forgiven. Under intense diplomatic pressure, a judicial hearing was called, but the French ambassador refused to participate, citing the "Laws of Nations," and instead demanded summary punishment of Bullock by the republic.

To really understand the situation, one must also put things into perspective. Today, 29 million Texans share 268,597 square miles, but back in 1840, the state was more than 100,000 square miles bigger, and there were only 70,000 people dividing up the whole enchilada. Austin's population in 1840 came in at a whopping 856 souls. Not the lowest of numbers, but this was still a very small town. These folks knew each other well, and every single one of them surely had some connection with Bullock and his family, who for years had welcomed all to their home and inn at the center of town.

As the locals were unwilling to sacrifice one of their own over the spite of a foreign diplomat yet wanting to salvage the relationship with the powerful and potentially generous ally, the compromise struck was to give a slap on the wrist to Bullock. This simply wasn't good enough for Alphonse, who wanted to see the full force of the law come to bear on his behalf.

Without any authorization from the home office, the French chargé d'affaires to the Republic of Texas abruptly cut diplomatic ties. He packed up his personal possessions from the nearly complete Legation and left the country for New Orleans. While there, he continued to loudly speak out against any French support to Texas. As a result, the deal he'd spent so much time and effort on was killed in the Senate, much like the hogs in his yard. Though publicly in support of their ambassador, de Saligny fell out of favor with his superiors, and his political influence waned after the incident. Before long, he was recalled back to France, where he lived out his days complaining about Texas the whole time.

Though it seems like this little story is just a private, if overblown, quarrel between two people long ago, the consequences continue to reverberate even today. With the loss of support from France, the idea of joining the

American Union became more realistic and perhaps even pushed Texas into a new relationship with the United States. The contributions Texans have made to the American story since annexation are immeasurable and would come to impact the entire world stage. Without Texas under its influence, France never regained its foothold in North America, and eventually its own ambitions of empire began to fade. These are some undeniably world-shaping events when it's all said and done, and it all came to pass over an argument about some hungry pigs.

EBENEZER THIRD BAPTIST CHURCH

1010 East 10th Street
Ebenezer Baptist Church is a traditionally Black church that has long been at the center of the East Side African American community. It was organized by Reverend C. Ward in 1875. The laws of the time prevented gatherings of these recently emancipated slaves, so Elisa Hawkins opened her home to the eighteen charter members of the fellowship. Soon they had built their first frame structure, but the congregation quickly outgrew it. By 1885, the first brick building, complete with stained-glass windows and a church bell, was constructed. It was then that history records a church member suggested the name "Ebenezer" because it means "stone of help." The name was adopted, and the congregation grew, adding a stucco tabernacle to the site in 1915. There was another major period of expansion for the church that lasted from 1950 to 1955, when the current Gothic-style church sanctuary, a parsonage and a new educational center were constructed. The bell that still peals from the tower is a relic of the original church.

Speaking of musical sounds for a moment, Ebenezer Baptist Church is renowned for its choir. Under the near lifelong leadership of music director and composer Virgie Carrington-Dewitty, the choir was catapulted to fame. The first major attention it received was when *The Bright and Early Choir* took over the airwaves as the first commercially sponsored radio program directed by a person of color. Virgie's education started in these church buildings and took her on to Tillotson College, the American Conservatory of Music in Chicago and even Juilliard School of Music in New York City, just to name a few. She and her husband stayed true to their lifelong commitments of using their extensive talents and education for the betterment of Austin. Her published songs number over sixty. Her

Ebenezer Baptist Church was organized in 1875 and is still central to the East Austin community.

list of honors and achievements, such as becoming the music director of the National Baptist Convention of America, is impressive on its own, much less in the context of her young adult life having been spent in the thick of Jim Crow–era laws, as well as the harsh reality of racial segregation in the education system that she thrived in both as a student and as an educator.

Check out the church website for details on visiting the campus or for information on how to hear a performance of the famed sanctuary choir.

TEXAS MUSIC HISTORY MUSEUM

1009 East 11th Street
The Texas Music History Museum is an all-volunteer organization that was created by local music lovers and aficionados in 1984. With some quick work, the group received its nonprofit status in 1985 and by 1986 had been recognized as a State Sesquicentennial Program for its mission of

"highlighting the contributions of Texas musicians to the musical heritage of the nation and the world."

In 1987, the board of directors developed a multigenre agenda for research, the creation of exhibitions and music programs. The exhibits, for the most part, are set up for hitting the road, and they make appearances with their mobile museum whenever an appropriate opportunity arises.

In 2003, the museum took up residence at the Marvin C. Griffin Building, allowing for a more visible and permanent presence to the archives and traveling displays. As you visit the small space and chat with the friendly, knowledgeable docents, you'll be astounded at the depth of their collection and the impact that Texas music has had all across the globe. Covering nearly every conceivable style of music, this collection includes photos, artifacts, costumes, interviews, posters and so much more. Check out the website for operating hours or to make a donation to the foundation.

DR. CHARLES URDY PLAZA AND THE *RHAPSODY* MOSAIC

1021 East 11th Street

Dr. Charles Urdy Plaza is a small corner lot with a brick clock tower and a large mosaic wall that sits on East 11th Street, welcoming all who would care to pause and reflect on the history of East Austin.

The mosaic wall piece, called *Rhapsody*, was created in 2003 by UT art professor Dr. John Yancey as a way to bring attention to the storied history of the East Side, especially East 11th Street, as the heart of the city's Black community. During this modern experience of cultural shifts and sweeping gentrification, Dr. Yancey wanted to create a permanent visual record of the place that served as a sanctuary and a home to the African American people who lived here and provided the backdrop to a vital part of our city's heritage.

The colorful mosaic features flowing patterns that sweep in and out of the fifty-foot-long installation and are inspired by West African masquerade rituals and traditional African American quilts. You'll notice it also depicts scenes of church, home, school, commerce and fraternity. Yancey describes these institutions as not just a part of Austin's Black community but as central to the identities of African American neighborhoods across the country. The children playing with the bicycle are sitting within a circle, which Dr. Yancey used to symbolize the safety found in the neighborhood.

Dr. Charles Urdy Plaza and *Rhapsody* mosaic commemorate the historic roots of the East Austin community.

Most prominent of all is the large scene of a band playing the music that would change America and the world—the very same music that would cross over the lines drawn by bigotry and segregation to soften the hearts of a nation: rock-and-roll. Austin has always been a place for the best up-and-coming musicians to entertain a crowd, and all the great forefathers and foremothers of rock-and-roll performed at clubs like the Victory Grill that were lined up and down East 11th Street.

One last note. A metaphor drawn from technicality, really. Most walls have a design that allows for lateral movement with the change of weather and the passing of time. This being a tile mosaic, that sort of surface change would have ruined the tiles, and the contractors building the wall had to engineer a totally different approach to provide the artwork a long life without allowing for that dangerous surface movement. The solution was to dig deep and build an extremely large foundation, as far as twenty feet below ground. Much like our history and shared communities, the part of the wall that stands above the ground is merely the tip of the iceberg, and the much larger part lies in its deeply held foundations. Not too bad, as far as metaphors go.

VICTORY GRILL

1104 East 11th Street

Already in view from Dr. Charles Urdy Plaza, the Victory Grill was the creation of local booking agent and band manager Johnny Holmes. The name is a reference to the fact that this famous spot opened to music lovers on "Victory over Japan Day" in 1945. This being the era of segregation, returning African American servicemen and musical acts with Black musicians couldn't just go anywhere to hear or play music, so clubs like the Victory Grill created the Austin leg of the "Chitlin Circuit," where performers like Etta James, Ray Charles, Ella Fitzgerald, Fats Domino and countless other giants of music cut their teeth touring in the days before their music was welcome in bars and on radios.

The venue actually began in a lean-to next to the larger building, but within a year, the business had grown enough to take over the main space, where we now see the murals of beloved musicians painted on the exterior walls. The shows were so popular that the enthralled crowds spilled out into the streets. Forget Dirty 6th Street. For decades, the heartbeat of

Mural on the side of the historic Victory Grill, one of the birthplaces of rock-and-roll in America.

American music could be heard right here. There was something different coming out of that club and the ones like it that ran along these blocks, and the people of the East Side came out in droves to get as close to the action as possible. "The street was so crowded you could barely walk. It was like New Orleans," one resident related.

In 1998, the Victory Grill was added to the National Register of Historic Places. Over the years, the business has opened and closed several times and is currently slated to make another comeback with a promise to honor its historic legacy and the crucial role it played in the evolution of American culture with the advent of rock-and-roll.

GEORGE WASHINGTON CARVER MUSEUM

1165 Angelina Street

The George Washington Carver Museum (GWCM) and the George Washington Carver Public Library are named for the famed African American inventor and scientist who did so much to advance humanity. The oldest building on this site is also the smallest at 1,720 square feet. The building was originally located downtown at the corner of 9th Street and Guadalupe and served as the main library branch for the city for eleven years. In 1933, the city chose to physically move the building to its present location to operate as a library for the Black community after the 1928 Master Plan had been enacted.

In the 1970s, a successful grassroots campaign was bringing attention to the lack of resources available to communities of color in Austin. We see this change of attitude reflected in the history of Austin's relationship with the area called Clarksville. This era also brought about the first site expansion to this library, which was completed in 1980. That same year, it was decided that the original building would be perfect to house the first museum in Texas dedicated to Black history.

In 1992, the museum created a three-phase, $11.5 million plan to develop the building we see today. Just over ten years later, in 2005, that dream was fully realized with this thirty-six-thousand-square-foot space that offers four art galleries, a dance studio, a photo lab and dark room for its community programs, classrooms, archive space, a 134-seat theater and, of course, a museum gift shop.

The adjacent library also received an expansion of fifteen thousand square feet, adding new meeting and study rooms, an art gallery,

George Washington Carver Museum Main Building, dedicated to the history of the Black communities of Austin and Texas.

George Washington Carver Genealogy Center. Also, Austin's first main library moved to this location in 1933.

EAST AUSTIN

computer labs and a youth library. Today, the GWCM collects and maintains books, maps, manuscripts, interviews and other materials in its efforts to document the African American experience in the New World throughout time.

In addition to its extensive community programs and educational offerings, the museum also hosts up to eleven major exhibitions each year, focusing on both history and culture. Check out its website for operating hours and its events calendar, and be sure to attend one of the many performances and productions.

UNIVERSITY OF TEXAS AT AUSTIN

UT AUSTIN

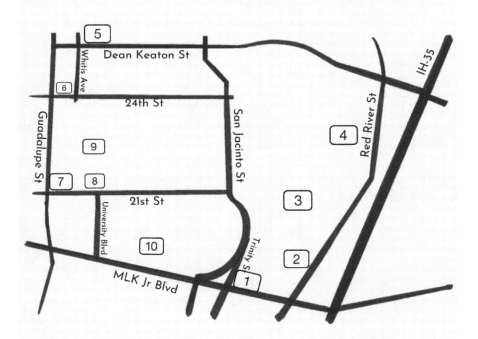

1. SANTA RITA WELL #1
2. TEXAS MEMORIAL STADIUM
3. TEXAS MEMORIAL MUSEUM
4. LBJ PRESIDENTIAL LIBRARY
5. MOODY COLLEGE OF COMMUNICATION
6. LITTLEFIELD HOME
7. HARRY RANSOM CENTER
8. LITTLEFIELD FOUNTAIN
9. UT TOWER AND MAIN BUILDING
10. BLANTON MUSEUM OF ART

The University of Texas is nothing less than its own town inside of the city of Austin. Covering 431 acres on the main campus, the school is the home of more than fifty thousand students and twenty-four thousand staff members. The eighteen different schools and colleges available to students at the university take up some twenty-two million square feet inside of 160 buildings and counting. One might think such an operation would be a burden on Austin's resources, but in fact, this institution is quite self-sufficient, complete as it is with its own power plant to heat, cool and power every building on campus, all on one of the world's largest micro-grids.

Suffice it to say that the history of UT is unbelievably rich, and the exploits of its more than 428,000 alumni not only deserve their own book but have already filled countless tomes.

SANTA RITA WELL #1

312 East Martin Luther King Jr. Boulevard
A campus of this size doesn't come cheap, and it has the vision of a man who's been mentioned more than once in this book, Governor Pease, to thank for it. It was he who had the foresight to set aside more than one million acres of land that could be leased out to endow a self-supporting university system in Texas.

In the early twentieth century, America witnessed the dawn of the petroleum age, when extremely large and productive deposits of oil and gas would be proven to exist in the vast wastelands of West Texas. Fortunately for the system's Permanent Fund, much of that oil-rich land was owned by the universities. Between 1917 and 1919, some five thousand oil and gas exploration permits were issued by the General Land Office on university land. One of these wells was dubbed Santa Rita, in honor of the patron saint of impossible things, as a way to pay homage to a small, kindly group of nuns from New York who bought a share in the exploratory venture.

The well would prove to be a world-changing success, but not until the two drillers who lived on site had put in two and a half years of back-breaking labor. The task at hand was to keep a slapped-together rig piercing deeper and deeper into the parched Texas dirt, clay and stone. Despite the shoddy equipment, the two drilled all the way down to more than three thousand feet, in fact. At times during this trying ordeal, the men would be forced to go months without pay and even longer without any assistance from a crew of roughnecks. The work was body-wrecking, the heat was unbearable and the job seemed to never end.

Top: West-facing view of UT Austin campus with Memorial Stadium on left and UT Tower in center.

Bottom: Mustang sculpture on UT Austin campus.

Santa Rita Well #1, the pumpjack that started the Texas oil boom and funded Texas education.

Either luck or the blessing of the saint was on the drillers' side, and though dozens of wells drilled by rivals had already come up short in the region, early on May 27, 1923, these two men caught the first signs hinting that they were on the oil. They quickly shut down the drill and capped off the well. They put their heads together and made a plan before rushing off the property on their mission. By the end of the day, the two men had bought every lease that they could get their hands on, and they owned the rights to more than thirty neighboring permits. It was indeed the right move, because the next day, with no assistance from the drillers, the Santa Rita Well began to spew oil steadily. It rushed out in continual pulses that would crescendo into a spray that would often rise higher than the top of the drilling tower, as if the well was posing for a photo as the quintessential "gusher."

The numbers show just how tied to the oil and gas market the fortunes of the UT system can be. The first royalty check sent to the school in August 1923 was for a mere $516.53. In 2009, the general fund was $11 billion. In 2018, it had risen to $19.5 billion, and just one year later, in 2019, we see its value spike to a staggering $31 billion.

At the northeast corner of MLK Jr. Boulevard and Trinity Street we find the original pump jack that sat atop that first well for so many years. A pump jack is the iconic wood and steel rocking horse–like structure seen all over the Southwest. A pump jack's tireless rocking draws every possible drop of oil from the depths of the earth and to the surface for processing and use. In its retirement, Santa Rita #1, as it came to be known, was refurbished and relocated to UT Austin's campus to serve as an outdoor museum piece and to pay homage to the history of energy production that fueled this university to such great heights.

DARRELL K. ROYAL TEXAS MEMORIAL STADIUM

405 East 23rd Street

Oil isn't the only moneymaker for the school. Athletics has also come to turn a tidy profit for the university coffers. As we continue up Trinity Street, one structure clearly holds court above all the other surrounding buildings. This is the absolutely massive home of the UT Longhorns football team, the Texas Memorial Stadium.

Darrell K. Royal Texas Memorial Stadium, the home of Longhorn football.

Created in 1924 at the suggestion of coaches and students, this gargantuan concrete structure has expanded from its original 24,000 seats to an official capacity in 2019 of 101,119. Numbers like that make this the largest of the Big 12 conference facilities, the eighth-largest stadium in the country and the ninth-largest stadium in the world. The attendance record is even higher and was set during a 2018 football game between UT and the University of Southern California, with 103,597 fans in attendance. Considering the 76.4 percent win ratio when the Longhorns have the home field advantage, it's no surprise that the game was won by UT 34–14.

The athletic program has excelled at creating profits from the school's investment. The men's athletic program has an enormous budget in excess of $43 million and returns more than $131 million in revenue. The attention to the athletic programs not only rakes in the cash but also serves as a major recruitment tool for potential students and pays off in accolades, championships and medals. The school boasts 53 national championships since 1949 and 517 regular season conference titles, and over 130 Olympic medals have been earned by student athletes. Don't let yourself think it's only about sports to these students, though. UT has also hosted 9 student athlete Rhodes Scholars.

TEXAS MEMORIAL MUSEUM

2400 Trinity Street
In the 1910s, UT faculty began alerting people that the East Coast institutions were taking specimens out of Texas due to the lack of collection facilities in the state. Not much was done on the matter by the powers that be; however, those in the know felt strongly that this was a major disservice to the state and continued to sound the alarm. In the 1920s, Professor F.L. Whitney of the University of Texas wrote, "If a Texas student or professor of Geology has need to examine a specimen of Dimetrodon, found ONLY in Texas Permian beds, he would have to visit a museum in Chicago, Michigan, or the East."

In the early 1930s, two professors from UT's anthropology and history departments joined forces in the creation of such a museum and spearheaded this cause. Timing was on the side of the museum, and as Texas barreled towards its centennial celebrations, the idea that we still hadn't built a state museum was becoming an embarrassment that would

Texas Memorial Museum's Art Deco entrance.

quickly translate into the political will needed to undertake the effort. All the pieces of the puzzle were now on the table, and when you put it all together, you get the Texas Memorial Museum.

On June 11, 1936, President Franklin D. Roosevelt made a campaign stop in Austin to rally the vote and attended the groundbreaking ceremony for the museum while he was in town. He even had the honor of setting off the first batch of dynamite to help start the project off with a bang.

Opening day, January 15, 1939, was far less explosive but still well attended by people excited to glimpse the new building that stands 75 feet high, 116 feet long and another 80 feet wide. The limestone construction with its decorative brass doors is reflective of the Art Deco style that is so often found in 1930s architecture such as this. Sadly, the museum has never lived up to its originally envisioned design that called for adding additional wings onto both sides of the building.

In 1959, the ownership and management of the collection was transferred from the state, which still plays a part in its funding, to the University of Texas. The school strives to create and maintain a space welcoming of all Texans, and it seems to work. Though a modest six hundred visitors came to the museum in 1949, annual guest counts these days soar in excess of thirty-five thousand.

The permanent exhibits are extensive, but they still only represent a tiny fraction of the more than five million pieces in the museum's collection of biological, geological, anthropological and historical artifacts and specimens. Check out the website for details on how best to plan your visit.

LBJ PRESIDENTIAL LIBRARY AND MEMORIAL FOUNTAIN

2313 Red River Street

Tucked behind and towering above the stately trees of UT sits the fourteen-acre campus of the Lyndon Baines Johnson Presidential Library, the LBJ School of Public Affairs and the LBJ Fountain. This monolithic tower made of travertine limestone serves as a sort of architectural metaphor for the thirty-sixth president of the United States. Seen from afar, this special stone shines in the sunlight and appears almost featureless, but as you get closer, you notice that it's actually covered with the pockmarks of ancient fossilized shells and other ocean creatures from a time, many eons ago, when this stone was ocean floor. Another example of architecture as metaphor is that a visitor enters this facility on what seems to be ground level but is actually the second floor. LBJ, too, was a man full of surprises and containing hidden depth and detail.

The impact that President Johnson had on Texas during his life and political career is hard to overstate. He casts a long shadow over the Lone Star State, even from the grave. With that in mind, it makes all the sense in the world that such an impressive monument in the form of a presidential library would be erected in his honor and that it would sit in Austin.

Early in his presidency, LBJ made an agreement with the federal government and the University of Texas to house and display the artifacts and documents of his time in office in a presidential library to be constructed in Austin. Johnson would provide the bulk of the collection's material; UT would construct and own the building and the federal government would operate the museum and maintain the collection into perpetuity.

Though many of the original features and displays remain, the library and museum received a major overhaul and upgrade with a multimillion-dollar renovation in 2012, breathing new life into the history of an important era of the twentieth century. The updated museum retains some longtime favorites, such as an animatronic LBJ telling his favorite jokes, but in the remodel, the curators also harnessed modern technology in clever ways to interact with museumgoers exploring the many displays and exhibits.

A view of the monolithic LBJ Presidential Library on UT Austin campus.

As usual, the museum is only able to present a small fraction of the full collection for viewing. The library holds some 54,000 objects, a mind-blowing 45 million pages of records, 650,000 photos and more than 1 million feet of videotape. There are 5,000 hours of recordings, 643 hours of which are telephone recordings and were almost always made without permission of the other person on the line. During his public career, LBJ recorded literally thousands of calls, and he kept personal possession of all the tapes until their donation to the library.

As a historical footnote, it does seem odd that LBJ could get away with a near decade-long wiretapping program when history painted the rather similar behavior of the next man to sit in the Oval Office in a very different light.

During Nixon's congressional impeachment woes, there was a fight to gain control of those secret tapes that were automatically made every time a phone receiver was picked up around Nixon. The embattled president was quick to point out that he'd inherited the idea of recording the calls from his predecessor. In an affidavit, Mr. Nixon testified, "President Johnson said that the recordings he had made of his conversations while President had proved to be exceedingly valuable in preparing his memoirs and he urged that [we] reinstall the recording devices." He went on to explain, "Thereafter, I consented that this be done, having the expectation that I, like President Johnson, could retain during my life exclusive control over access to the recordings." Unfortunately for him, Congress saw the tapes differently, and the incident led to Nixon's infamous resignation.

The LBJ Presidential Library was dedicated on May 22, 1971, and during the ceremony, President Johnson was frank in his hopes and intentions for the endeavor when he remarked, "It is all here: the story of our time—with the bark off. This library does not say, 'This is how I saw it,' but, this is how the documents show it was. There is no record of a mistake, nothing critical, ugly, or unpleasant that is not included in the files here. We have papers from my forty years of public service in one place, for friend and foe to judge, to approve or disapprove. I do not know how this period will be regarded in years to come. But that is not the point. This library will show the facts—not just the joy and triumphs, but the sorrow and failures, too."

During the creation and planning period of the library, President Johnson and especially Lady Bird were personally and deeply involved in the design of the building and the curation of the collection. Lady Bird was always an extremely capable political partner for LBJ. She was said to have been the true mastermind of the library, and after their stint in the White House and the death of her husband, she spent more and more of her time here. In fact, Lady Bird maintained an office and lived in a hidden apartment on the tenth floor of this building for the rest of her life. After her death and the subsequent remodel in 2012, her office was preserved as an exhibit, and it is now open to visitors. It sits just steps away from the seven-eighths-scale replica of the Oval Office, both forever locked in time just as the rooms had been left.

President Johnson may not have known how history would come to judge him in hindsight, but the couple did have a sense of their place in history. The library's travertine limestone walls continue throughout the interior and are etched, inches deep, with Johnson's name and the symbols of his office. In the end, he certainly made his mark, as these carved words and seals are sure to outlive even our great society and will someday lie in wait for archaeologists of the future to rediscover and to inspire wonder about the man for whom it was dedicated and the nation that built it. Upon her death in 2007, Lady Bird, just like her husband, was laid in repose beneath the massive presidential seal in the great hall so a grieving world could come and pay their respects.

The stories and deeds of President and Mrs. Johnson are each woven into so many of the places, so much of the history and, most certainly, so many of the people of Austin. Be it the wildflowers that line our roadways, the creation of the power plants that feed our modern world, his ushering of civil rights legislation in a harshly divided and turbulent America or just a day out on the lake we call Lady Bird, the impact and influence of this family's indefatigable contributions will continue to reverberate in the Texas capital and beyond for generations to come.

MOODY COLLEGE OF COMMUNICATION

300 West Dean Keeton Street
The Moody College of Communication has its roots in the popular oratory classes that have been offered at UT since it opened in 1883. By 1899, the packed classrooms had grown into the Department of Public Speaking, now called the Department of Communication Studies. Over the decades since, additional schools and programs grew from that department, and in 1965, the School of Journalism, the Department of Speech and the Department of Radio-Television-Film officially organized together under the School of Communication. The 2000s heralded unprecedented growth for the college. The Department of Journalism became the School of Journalism, and construction began on the $54.8 million, 120,000-square-foot Belo Center, with its lecture halls, classrooms, studios and meeting spaces for up to 4,600 students that we see today. In 2013, after a breathtaking gift of $50 million was provided by the Moody Foundation, it was renamed the Moody College of Communication.

Like so many other colleges on the UT Austin campus, the sheer number of notable alumni is beyond impressive. The list has produced thirty-four Pulitzer Prizes, three Oscars and forty-two Emmys at present count.

The studios of KUT-FM, the ever-popular local NPR affiliate in Austin, are located in the Moody College of Communication, and the school has played a major role in its story since the station went on air in 1958. The station was an offshoot of a physics experiment in the early 1920s and is directly related to Penn Field, which we explored way back in the '04 District. By the end of World War I, the Defense Department funds had dried up and the cost of operating the station became too great for the UT Physics Department to shoulder on its limited budget. With that decided, the equipment was mothballed until the mid-1950s, when work

This skybridge over Dean Keeton connects buildings at UT's Moody College of Communication.

began behind the scenes to fund and license a radio station operated by the university's Communications Department.

Today, KUT 90.5 FM and its music-centric sister station, KUT-X, found at 98.9 on your FM dial, are among the highest-performing public radio stations in the country. With more than 250,000 listers tuning in each week, the station regularly sits at the top of the ratings while raking in the awards, such as its twenty-five regional and two national Edward R. Murrow Awards, along with seven National Headliners Awards, just to name a few.

On the television front, the Moody College of Communications has made countless contributions to American culture, but none has had more of an impact than the *Austin City Limits* PBS television show. *ACL* is a public television music program that began in 1974 and is produced in association with the local PBS station, KLRU. Willie Nelson was the first guest artist to air and has since become known locally as the "Patron Saint of Austin Music." The show, which took off like a rocket, was quickly syndicated around the globe. This long-lived, still-running and widely adored program was instrumental in presenting Austin as the "Live Music Capital of the World."

In 2003, *ACL* became the only television program to be awarded the National Medal of Art. In 2010, the show was inducted in the Rock and Roll Hall of Fame, and if the folks behind it all still hadn't gotten the point on how well respected their little production had become, in 2011, it was even given the rarely received and highly coveted Peabody Award for its work preserving and presenting American music.

Over the first thirty-six seasons, the show was taped on the UT campus, in Studio 6A of Communications Building B, which it made famous. The diminutive space could only safely seat three hundred, so standing in line for a chance through the doors was a favorite pastime of many an Austinite, and for many years the tradition continued.

On February 26, 2011, *ACL Live* underwent its biggest change to date when it taped the first-ever show from the spacious comfort of its new purpose-built home at the Moody Theatre. The new, multimillion-dollar, state-of-the-art, 2,750-seat theater is part of the upscale Block 21 complex on 2nd Street in downtown Austin. You'll know you've arrived when you see the statue of Willie Nelson out front.

LITTLEFIELD HOME

302 West 24th Street

Hidden among the Moody College buildings and sitting at the northwest corner of Whitis Avenue and 24th Street, we find the stately and most historic Littlefield Home.

Littlefield is a name often seen on buildings around Austin. The family that bears the name owes the seeds of their fortune to the family patriarch, George Washington Littlefield. Born in 1842 to a family with wealth by means of a slave-run plantation, George went off at a young age to seek an education, a bit of adventure and, of course, his own fortune. Though he had a brief stop at Baylor University, his first taste of the real world was accompanied by the sounds, the smells and the agony of battle.

Littlefield joined the Confederate rebellion in the Civil War, and by the tender young age of twenty, he'd received a battlefield promotion to captain and was voted to command his company in the Battle of Shiloh. This led to further advancement, more battles and eventually to his inability to walk without the use of a cane for years after the war had ended. His time on the battlefield would shape George for the rest of his life, and among other things, he would commit himself to preserving the memory of the men he fought alongside.

Back in Texas during the Reconstruction era, it took George some time to catch his luck, as he floundered through his first seasons of farming, with

The historic Littlefield House, home to one of UT Austin's most loyal patron families and located on campus.

three straight years of blight and floods nearly pushing him to the brink of bankruptcy. Trying a different tack, he took a risk on speculating the cattle market and became one of the many cowboys pushing dogies up from Texas to the bustling meatpacking districts of Kansas.

A lot of cowboys at the time didn't want to risk their own hard-earned money buying cows that might die on the long trail to the cattle markets, but they would hire themselves out to the ranchers and do the drive on their behalf for a fee. Littlefield was a hands-on guy, so he purchased cattle up front from the ranchers on the cheap and assumed all the risk of personally transporting them to market, reaping all the profits for himself in the process. Building off his initial success, Littlefield opened up a profitable dry goods store, and he began purchasing ranches and water rights all over the Southwest. Soon, he established his own large herds of cattle, cutting out the ranchers, too. These herds were grazing on plots of land so big that one of them out-measured the state of Rhode Island.

With unparalleled business success now firmly in his grasp, and with capital pouring in from all directions, Littlefield relocated his family to Austin in 1883 and entered the ever-profitable world of banking. By 1890, he had organized the American National Bank and served as its president until 1919, which was the year preceding his death. It was during this era that he built this home, as well as one of the first high-rise buildings in downtown, which is still known as the Littlefield Building. He even took possession of the famous Driskill Hotel from 1895 to 1903, which was when the hotel received its signature bank vault in the lobby, as well as the installation of electric lighting.

By the early 1900s, he had turned his philanthropic sights to UT. The attention was most fortunate for the university. At one point, Littlefield committed himself to covering the entire budget for the briefly defunded college out of his own pocket. While he served as a university regent, he tapped into his vast fortune to build classrooms, dormitories and many Civil War memorials that have since been removed by the university to better suit the changing attitudes toward race in the modern South and in hopes of eliminating any obstacle to inclusion and diversity on campus.

UT will remain indebted to the Littlefield family for their generosity in providing such a constant lifeline to the school during its toughest times, but the family still had yet another gift for the campus, which was the donation of this bespoke Victorian-style home upon the death of Mrs. Littlefield in 1935. The home was added to the National Register of Historic Places in 1970 and today is used as office space. With the University of Texas caring for the property, it's sure to be here for many generations to come.

HARRY RANSOM CENTER

300 West 21st Street

Welcome to the Harry Ransom Center, a safe space for media collections of all types and from all over the world. From the first photograph ever taken (which, if you can believe it, *wasn't* a selfie) to one of only twenty complete copies of the Gutenberg Bible still in existence, this eclectic collection is absolutely astounding.

The center was founded in 1957 by Harry Ransom, a visionary English professor whose career would eventually see him rise all the way up to the position of university chancellor. In a speech a year before its creation, he shared his vision of "a center of cultural compass, a research center to be the Bibliothèque Nationale of the only state that started out as an independent nation." The university rallied around the idea, and in short order, it jumpstarted the center with the contents of three large collections, including one that was procured on the request of the college by that now familiar benefactor, George Littlefield.

In addition to being a place of protection and study for the word's media collection, the center also strives to "provide unique insight into the creative process," which it accomplishes by creating rotating exhibits drawn from the more than 1 million books, more than 42 million manuscripts, 5 million photographs and 100,000 works of art that are deposited behind the scenes. This collection is beyond extensive. In it, you'll find three copies of the First *Folio of William Shakespeare* (1623), a suppressed first edition of *Alice's Adventures in Wonderland*, paintings by Pablo Picasso and Frida Kahlo, sets used by Salvador Dali in *Spellbound* and costumes and production materials from *Gone with the Wind*. There's Kerouac's diary from his time writing *On the Road* and Edgar Allan Poe's actual writing desk. There's even a tarot deck hand-painted by Aleister Crowley, the king of the modern occult himself. The collection is virtually inexhaustible, and no matter where your interests lie, you're sure to find more than a few things that pique your curiosity at the Ransom Media Center.

LITTLEFIELD FOUNTAIN

201 West 21ˢᵗ Street

Our next stop is the Littlefield Fountain, sometimes referred to as the Littlefield Gate, and it again harkens back to that very same George Littlefield who we've been discussing in this chapter. The fountain, as it's seen today, is a shadow of its former self, and even that was a shadow the original and rather grand ambitions of Major Littlefield.

This war memorial, designed by celebrated Italian-born sculptor Pompeo Coppini, was completed in 1933, more than a decade after the first plans were made for its creation. The fountain is set into a three-tiered semicircular granite pool and backed with a limestone wall. Rising triumphantly above the water is a large bronze sculpture. It depicts a ship bearing the winged figure of Columbia, the female personification of the United States, standing on the prow. In each hand she raises a torch and flanking her on one side is a soldier and on the other a sailor. In front of the ship it gets really interesting, with three mighty hippocamps, a sort of horse mixed with a fish. These fish-steeds are emerging from the water, and the two outermost of them are being ridden by mermen. These mermen are taming the center hippocamps, each with a hand firmly grasping a portion of its mane to use as a rein.

View of Littlefield Fountain and UT Tower, built to be the "main gate" of campus.

The impetus for commissioning and funding the creation of the fountain and its sculpture was twofold for George Washington Littlefield. On the one hand, there was a competing benefactor in Austin named George Washington Breckinridge, and the two had little in common beyond their historic namesake. Breckinridge was a staunch Union man in the Civil War, a proponent of women's suffrage and education, as well as being sympathetic to the needs of the Black community in the Reconstruction era. With Littlefield's loyalties being what they were, it was nearly inevitable that the two magnates would never get along. In the major's view, his rival was trying to use his wealth to "northern-ize" UT while also attempting to lure the university campus away from the original forty acres adjacent to the Littlefield Home. The major saw his large donations, such as this fountain, as a way to continue holding sway over the university board and "nail it down," once and for all.

On the other hand, Littlefield had a deeply held desire to use his vast fortune to rewrite history as more favorable to the Confederate cause and to memorialize those who led and participated from the Southern states such as Texas. The Civil War was hard to let go of for many veterans, and this can be said especially for George Littlefield. To make the point, consider this: though he held many titles and positions in his lifetime he still never let go of the honorific he'd earned in war, his rank of major in the Confederate army, and with it the recognition of his glory days in the bloody battles like Shiloh.

In light of his motivation to reinvigorate the esteem in which his heroes were held by his community, the plans he requested from Coppini originally called for a large bronze arch bearing the faces and names of Rebel soldiers and leaders, along with the fountain and an additional six portrait statues of Rebel war leaders. This idea was controversial even for a Jim Crow–era Austin of the 1920s, which for the most part had long ago laid down its plans or hopes for a return to rebellion against the Union and saw any glorification of the conflict as untoward, if not worse.

The artist understood the vision he was being commissioned to bring to life, but he could also read the writing on the wall at the time. He pushed hard for a compromised version that would give Littlefield most of what he wanted but in a way that wouldn't grow more and more unwelcome on campus over time. As Littlefield had requested, the subjects of the portrait statues would remain, but Coppini attempted to recast the gateway as a war memorial honoring Texas soldiers in general. The prescient sculptor explained to Littlefield, "As time goes by, they will look to the Civil War as a blot on the pages of American history, and the Littlefield Memorial will be resented as keeping up the hatred between the Northern and Southern states." Instead, Coppini proposed to honor those who had fought in the World War, as "all past regional differences have disappeared, and we are now one welded nation." With the point made, Coppini presented his revised plan for the project.

The artist was correct in his take on the way things would progress in America. Between the years 2015 to 2017, after decades of calls to action from students and civil rights activists that began with the fountain's opening, UT began removal of the six portrait statues, as well as the Confederate names carved into the fountain's walls. UT has gone on to remove other sculptures commemorating the era across campus. Some of these removed pieces were donated to organizations that protect southern American heritage, and others will go to museums displays on campus when appropriate.

Though the fountain has flowed with as much controversy as it has water, the amended version of the memorial has remained a centerpiece of UT as it gives entrance to the Quad that sits between the fountain and the UT Tower and Main Building. It remains a beloved landmark steeped in its own traditions and the gateway to the campus.

UT TOWER AND MAIN BUILDING

110 Inner Campus Drive

The most visible, recognizable and iconic symbol of the UT campus is the 307-foot, twenty-seven-floor UT Tower. This structure was one of ten on campus built by designer Paul Cret and was finished in 1937, which was just in time for the university's fiftieth anniversary. Originally used as a closed-stack library, today the building houses administration offices, study rooms and the Life Sciences Library.

In 1955, there was an incident on the UT campus that shook the world, and it was centered on the tower. For more than an hour, shots rang out across the campus as a twenty-five-year-old former marine and former UT engineering student named Charles Whitman went on a murderous rampage from the observation deck atop the UT Tower. Many books and several documentary films have been made in an effort to understand what occurred that day, in what would be the worst mass shooting for many years to take place in Texas and one of the first on a school campus in America, though it would sadly not be the last.

Whitman was an all-American sort of guy on the outside. He mastered the piano early and was one of the youngest ever to earn Eagle Scout in the history of the Boy Scouts. Born to an abusive, perfectionist father, none of Charles's early accomplishments seemed to impress him much, except one. His father was always the proudest of his son's expert marksmanship, and so Charles pursued it even more. Seeing a way out of his troubled home, Charles Whitman would go on to serve in the U.S. Marine Corps. There, he would rise among the ranks as a sharpshooter before attending UT as an engineering student on a naval scholarship. Soon his grades slipped, a deal-breaker for his scholarship, and as a result he was recalled as an enlisted man. His return to active duty was short-lived, and he was discharged from service and returned to Austin.

The shooter didn't survive his spree, so we'll never truly know what motivated him, but he did leave a lengthy suicide note. From that final letter we know that after a year of "overwhelming, violent impulses" that included intense fantasies about shooting people from the tower, he also wrote of experiencing extremely severe headaches. In his attempt to explain his actions, he mentions seeking help but that he also didn't return for treatment and was never able to remedy his complaints on his own. We also know in his suicide note that Whitman himself suggested an autopsy be performed, believing it might produce something of interest. He was right; the postmortem procedure did in fact show a hypothalamic tumor present. This region of the anatomy includes the little-understood parts of the brain involved with hormone production and can be heavily influential in terms of behavior.

We also know the actions of this man were not passion induced, as he began his activities the night before he went to the tower, in his own home, with the killing of his mother and then his wife. He said he killed them to spare them the suffering of living with the acts he intended to commit the next day, demonstrating that he was clearly aware of the gravity of his intentional path toward death. Whitman also stopped by the bank in the morning, several hours after his first two acts of murder, so he could bounce some bad checks and use the money at the gun store, where he stopped by last so he could increase his arsenal and purchase more ammunition.

What followed was beyond terrifying for the victims. In a crime scene that spanned the five city blocks at the center of campus, fourteen people were killed and another thirty-one were injured. Some of the injuries were quite severe and left the victims disabled for the rest of their lives. The horror of that day marked an awakening from an age of innocence. *Time* magazine marked the event as the second-most important story of the year, with only news from the Vietnam War weighing heavier on the hearts and minds of Americans.

Many heroes masquerading as normal people were revealed on that fateful day. With no idea where the gunfire was coming from, friends and strangers alike risked and too often lost their lives to help those who had been struck from out of nowhere and were still in harm's way. The conflict ended when two police officers and the deputized manager of a local store climbed the tower's exterior to gain access to the holed-up shooter who had come prepared for a long siege. In a close-quarters exchange of fire, Charles Whitman was killed.

From that point on, Austin, along with the rest of the world, has struggled to understand what could twist one of our own into such an unrecognizable monster. We've created memorial spaces, studied the available materials and searched our own hearts lest the same bitter seeds take root again. Over the years of healing and recovery, the UT Tower has been reclaimed by Austinites and by the university. Today, it stands as a symbol of unity, a symbol of the search for knowledge and a reminder of the rewards of fraternity, just as it always had before that fateful day.

BLANTON MUSEUM OF ART

200 East Martin Luther King Jr. Boulevard

The Blanton Museum of Art is the proud new repository of UT's vast permanent collection of art. With roots that stretch back to the early 1960s, a time when UT's permanent art collection was split between the Art Department and the Ransom Center, the Blanton Museum of Art didn't finally come into its own until 2006, when this facility opened its doors with a twenty-four-hour marathon celebration.

The 189,249-square-foot building is now the home of UT Austin's permanent art collection that holds more than eighteen thousand pieces of art these days, and it's still growing. You'll find artistic treasures that include classical European paintings, prints, drawings and sculpture, as well as contemporary American and Latin American pieces. The facility also boasts room for its permanent collection galleries, temporary exhibits, archival storage, offices, classrooms, print study rooms, an auditorium, a café and, of course, a gift shop.

Admission to the Blanton also includes access to a special permanent installation on the site. In the plaza outside the museum sits a large, somewhat plain-looking, double-barrel-vaulted Romanesque structure made of Spanish limestone. The famed contemporary artist who gifted UT the plans for this structure called *Austin* was Ellsworth Kelly. It was the last, and perhaps the most ambitious, work of his life. With this piece, he followed in a tradition of contemporary artist–commissioned structures such as the Matisse Chapel. The plans were drawn up and given to the

Ellsworth Kelly's final work, *Austin,* a temple-like structural art piece located in the plaza of UT's Blanton Museum of Art.

university, and it raised $15 million and happily built the structure. In 2018, *Austin* opened to visitors.

As you view this building, you'll quickly note that the eastern, southern and western walls, or the sun-facing walls, each hold different-sized, shaped, colored and positioned stained-glass window panels. You'll also note that each of these is arranged into its own geometric pattern. In fact, there are thirty-three of these handblown glass panes at this temple of sorts.

Inside this mysterious structure, after passing through the massive carved wooden doors hewn from a live oak tree that was harvested from the building site of UT's Dell Medical Center, the visitor is struck by the spartan appearance of the chapel-like room. In fact, some of the only things inside, aside from the docent, are fourteen black and white marble panels lining the walls, said to be Ellsworth's contemporary take on the stations of the cross. There is one other object inside, and to find it, look to the north end of the room that features an alcove instead of windows. In this domed nook that in a church would perhaps display a cross, we find one of the finest examples of the wooden totemic pieces that Kelly had long explored in his work.

Falling onto walls and the stone slabs that make up the floor, you see the true subject of this epic and immersive piece is the multicolored light pouring in from the window panels above. The constantly changing interplay of sun through colored panes creates an ever-shifting palette of hues that spill around the room. The change occurs in nearly imperceptibly slow motion, giving the viewer a false sense of stability to the look of the space. That illusion would be shattered with a second visit at another time of day or year, when the light would paint the room in an entirely different way. It's as though your moment of interaction with this worship of color and light is yours alone, never to be captured by another viewer in exactly the same way again, much like your exploration of Austin.

DOWNTOWN AUSTIN

DOWNTOWN

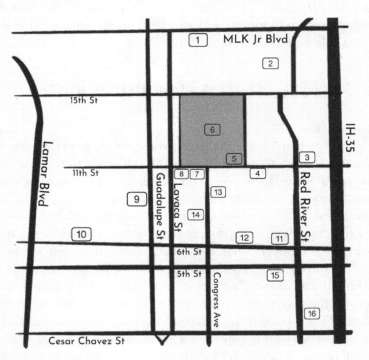

1. TEXAS STATE HISTORY MUSEUM
2. SCHOLZ GARTEN
3. SYMPHONY SQUARE
4. MOONLIGHT TOWERS
5. CAPITOL VISITORS CENTER
6. TEXAS STATE CAPITOL
7. OLD CAPITOL RUINS
8. TEXAS GOVERNOR'S MANSION
9. BREMOND BLOCK
10. WEST 6th STREET
11. DIRTY 6th STREET
12. DRISKILL HOTEL
13. PARAMOUNT THEATRE
14. SAVIOR OF AUSTIN STATUE
15. O. HENRY MUSEUM
16. MOONSHINE GRILL

We now turn our attention to downtown Austin, ever a center of activity for Austinites, and also the undisputed center of our history. As we've noted throughout this adventure, for many generations of Austinites, downtown wasn't "Downtown"; it was just the town. The population of town was concentrated in this area for generations, and it wasn't until early in the twentieth century that growth required expansion outside the original boundaries of the town and into the surrounding hills and farmlands.

The historical offerings in this area are densely packed and span every era. As in other parts of town that we've seen, here we'll visit some of the most significant and interesting destinations while keeping in mind that there's a whole lot more where this came from.

BOB BULLOCK TEXAS STATE HISTORY MUSEUM

1800 Congress Avenue

There's hardly a better place to dive into downtown than where we last left off. Across the street from the Blanton Art Museum, you'll find the Bob Bullock Texas State History Museum. Dedicated to presenting the ever-evolving "Story of Texas" in engaging and interesting ways, the Bullock Museum takes on the Texas-sized task of sharing the infinitely faceted tale of the Lone Star State. The nine million annual visitors to the museum get to explore a history that dates back more than sixteen thousand years—from the earliest traces of the first Native peoples to call this place home through the days of settlement, rebellion and the founding of the republic, all the way to the space age and beyond. As you wind through the museum's twists and turns, you'll see how the people of this land have impacted, touched and inspired the entire world in one way or another. The building was designed to lead the visitor along three immersive levels of exhibits and interactive displays. Along the way, you'll be transported through the pivotal moments of our history.

There's certainly a lot to take in while you're here, but don't miss the fascinating temporary exhibits that change two or three times a year on the ground level. Adjacent to that exhibit space you'll find the entrance to the permanent collection, and right away you'll be face to face with one of the museum's greatest treasures: a large, mostly reassembled portion of the once sunken and now recovered French sailing ship *La Belle*. This was one of three ships under the command of the explorer

Texas star in front of Bob Bullock Texas State History Museum at the northern entrance to the Texas Mall.

La Salle before the ships were caught in a storm and claimed by the sea. Rediscovered off the Texas coast in the Gulf of Mexico, the vessel and its many artifacts have been salvaged from the depths. Each piece has been painstakingly pried from the grasp of ocean mud and eventually made its way here to be studied, preserved and meticulously placed as this centerpiece of the museum. This ship's misfortune is the history lover's delight!

As you stroll through the museum, you'll witness for yourself the view from Stephen F. Austin's jail cell in Mexico City in a complete re-creation and walk along the cobblestone streets of the 1800s. You'll stand on faithful reproductions of the cotton-laden piers of Galveston Harbor at the turn of the twentieth century, set your gaze upon the *Goddess of Liberty* statue that originally sat atop the capitol and engage all of your senses in the 5-D Texas Spirit Theatre. All of that and more awaits you at the one and only Bob Bullock Texas State History Museum. Be sure to check its website for hours, showtimes and ticketing prices.

SCHOLZ GARTEN

1607 San Jacinto Boulevard

Founded in 1866, Scholz Garten stands proud as the oldest operating business in all of Texas and the oldest beer garden in America. It's so fantastically old that General Custer would drink here to get away from his camp at what is now Pease Park during the Reconstruction era. Things went downhill for Custer when he left Austin. Perhaps he should have stayed for one more round of beer and schnitzel. Cowboys, outlaws, celebrities, politicians, UT students who would go on to change the world—this place has seen it all.

Simply put, you just don't get this kind of longevity unless you're doing something right, and this place does everything right. More than just a beer joint, the menu reveals the deep ties this business has to the area's large German community and its rich heritage. Along with their savory menu, the settlers also brought along their traditions, their sports and their music

This music staff sitting above Scholz Garten and Saengerrunde Halle hints at this building's musical story, past and present.

to Central Texas. This influence included traditional German singing clubs, such as the Austin Saengerrunde. By the early 1900s, the choir was so deeply ingrained in life at the bar that the group purchased the space in 1908.

The singing club begat other clubs such as the Saengerrunde Bowling Club, which built the six-lane bowling alley next to the popular covered outdoor Beergarten. This bowling center is one of the oldest continually running bowling alleys in America and one of the last lanes in the country to not be electrified. The pins have to be reset by hand even today. Ask to check it out for yourself when you pop in for a round and soak in the history.

SYMPHONY SQUARE

1111 Red River Street
We find our next stop at the northeast corner of 11th Street and Red River Street. It's a stone construction that today is the home of the Austin Symphony Orchestra and is called Symphony Square. Austin has employed a professional symphony orchestra since 1911, one of the longest runs for an orchestra in the whole country and especially impressive when you consider that most of our population growth is a fairly recent occurrence. For the bulk of our orchestra's more than one-hundred-year history, it was playing for a rather modest-sized town. What Austin lacked in size, it more than made up for in enthusiastic support of the fine arts, and in the decades since, the Austin Symphony Orchestra has always maintained its status as a treasured part of our city experience.

In 1971, preservation-minded citizens began rallying support for a plan that would turn historic structures such as this unique triangular stone home, said to be one of three such structures still standing in Texas, into something that would safeguard the building and, from it, support a community resource such as the orchestra.

Before its career in music as an office space and 350-seat amphitheater, this building began life as a home constructed by Representative Jeremiah Hamilton, a much-revered Black political and civic leader in Texas. Hamilton was born in 1838 and was brought to Texas as a slave in 1847 when he was nine years old. He became literate as a slave and established one of the earliest schools for Black students soon after the Civil War. In Reconstruction, already a spokesman for African American causes, he acquired land in Bastrop County and then served as a land trustee for others like him emerging from the grips of slavery. He successfully ran for a seat in

Symphony Square is located in this unique triangular stone building constructed by one of Texas's first African American legislators, Jeremiah Hamilton.

the Texas House of Representatives and was one of nine Black legislators who served in the Twelfth Texas Legislature from 1869 to 1871.

After his term in the Texas House of Representatives, Jeremiah Hamilton remained in Austin, working mostly as a carpenter and building this home for his large family in 1871. Age was pressing on him by the mid-1880s. With his health no longer allowing him to make a living in his trade, he made a move into the newspaper business and became owner and editor of the *Austin Citizen*. By the 1890s, he owned the *National Union*, and then he also served as an agent to the *Austin Watchmen*. All three papers primarily catered to the interests and needs of the Black community. He remained active in civic affairs and a leader in politics throughout his life. This well-built structure, like Hamilton's legacy, still stands tall today. Check out the Austin Symphony Orchestra website for performance schedules and event listings to catch a glimpse inside this historic space.

THE AUSTIN MOONLIGHT TOWERS AND THE SERVANT GIRL ANNIHILATOR

For the first two decades of our settlement, Austinites lived in near total darkness after sunset. When evening shadows lengthened into blankets of inky black, real dangers lurked in the night. It's hard for our modern minds to truly imagine the psychological impact of experiencing that nightly ebony abyss while living on the edge of what these settlers considered to be civilization, but suffice it to say that the advent of sustained lighting across an entire city was heralded by those who lived in that moment as something near miraculous. By the 1860s, the citizenry of Austin favored the investment in gas lighting, and for the next two and a half decades, one company or another was given the contract to install and maintain gas-powered lamp posts. More than once, Austin would neglect to pay the bills, and the town would sink back into darkness. It may well have been one of those times of unpaid bills and unlit lamps that the person who is considered to be America's first serial killer began his bloody spree.

The nightmare began on December 30, 1884, with the killing of Mollie Smith. Mollie was a twenty-five-year-old woman of color who worked as a cook for a well-to-do family in town. She was found dead outside their home. The nets of suspicion were widely cast but never produced the killer. To qualify this, or any of these killings, with words such as *gruesome* would be to understate the startling violence that was unleashed on the city as of that night. The horrific wounds left on Mollie told a story of a murder done by axe and performed by a murderer bereft of remorse or conscience. The city shuddered at the act but tried to forget the carnage. They might have eventually succeeded, except that just five months after Mollie's death, on May 7, 1885, Eliza Shelly, another young Black woman who also worked as a cook for a local wealthy family, was found dead with wounds from repeated blows of an axe. The details of this new dark deed were disturbingly familiar, and it was clearly linked to Mollie's demise.

Moonlight towers over Austin were once a state-of-the-art lighting option; now they've become a symbol of Austin itself.

Sadly, and terrifyingly, the killer, known first as the "Austin Axe Murderer," was just getting started.

More death followed; each new victim and every additional crime scene clearly fit into these unique criteria. This was something more than random and something more disturbing than the crimes of passion or drunken ire that investigators had seen all too often before. These were acts of pure evil, and the deaths kept coming throughout 1885. Soon, William Sydney Porter (again we find the fingerprints on our history of the man who would later be known as O. Henry) said in a letter to a friend, "Town is fearfully dull, except for the frequent raids of the Servant Girl Annihilators, who make things lively during the dead of night." Once that missive got around, the term "Servant Girl Annihilator" became the preferred nickname for the killer in the headlines of the local and national press.

In a panic that swept the town, people rushed through their evening errands to make it home before sunset, where locks had been installed on once open doors. Saloons, usually operating twenty-four hours a day, closed by midnight, and neighborhood patrols increased, as did the death toll. Sometimes an innocent bystander who was near the intended victim at the moment of the attack would be killed or gravely wounded as the monster dragged his prey from their own beds and out into the darkness. After a year full of murders, the last of the killings came in a pair and seemed an assault on the gentry themselves. The killer had become emboldened perhaps by a planned departure, and on Christmas Eve 1885, Sue Hancock, this time not a servant but instead a socialite white woman and said to be "one of the most refined ladies in Austin," was found mutilated by axe in her yard. Mere hours later, unimaginably, a second report came through to police. Another victim, also a prominent white woman, Mrs. Eula Phillips, "one of the prettiest women in Austin," was found horrifically murdered in her yard just blocks away from the first murder. Husbands were suspected, as was everyone else. Over the course of this year from hell, more than four hundred men and women were arrested or detained on suspicion of involvement in the heinous crimes. The victims numbered eight dead, and another eight bystanders were gravely wounded by the time the row concluded.

Three years later, another serial killer would capture the attention of the world, one known infamously as Jack the Ripper. Some have suggested that perhaps the same man who was never apprehended for the murders in Austin could have gained passage to England via nearby Galveston Harbor, and after settling into life in London, he resumed his ghastly activities. As titillating as that possibility might be to a macabre imagination, the cold-case evidence seems to suggest that any connection between the two killers is little more than a far fetch or a tall tale.

What can be said with assurance is that an opportunity to continually and brightly illuminate the city in a way that wouldn't break the bank was understandably very attractive to local leaders at the end of the nineteenth century. In response to the need for safety, Austin made an early attempt at taming the Colorado River with the hydroelectric-generating Austin Dam, which they hoped would permanently bring new and superior electric lighting to the city of Austin for no more than the cost of construction and maintenance.

By 1894, nearly ten years after the murders, and with the dam's generators operational, a deal was struck with the City of Detroit, and Austin took possession of thirty-one "moonlight towers," each standing 165 feet above its 15-foot-deep foundations. Together, these strategically positioned lamps provided the entire city of fifteen thousand people with light as bright as a full moon, thus earning their name. It was so bright that the local citizens, new to such technology, feared that crop growing cycles would be altered, and some folks even took to carrying an umbrella around town at night to protect their skin from the electric rays. Others complained of disorientation due to the effects of having multiple shadows cast from the six powerful mercury vapor bulbs atop each tower.

In 1993, all of the towers were taken down and painstakingly refurbished and reconstructed down to the last bolt and guidewire. The $1.3 million restoration project should prolong the life of the towers by as much as fifty to seventy-five years. When the fifteen towers that survived the refits were placed back up on their perches, Austin did what it does best and threw a festival to celebrate.

Today, the moonlight towers in Austin are the last ones still in operation anywhere on earth, and our weird love of these lights and our commitment to their preservation makes perfect sense to the Austinite and is to us what the trolleys are to proud San Franciscans: a simple and enduring symbol of a frontier people taming the elements that would limit them. In San Francisco, it was about conquering the nearly impassable hills and terrain, and for Austin, it was about controlling the floods and bringing illumination to the dark, deadly night.

TEXAS STATE CAPITOL BUILDING VISITORS CENTER

112 East 11th Street
Any exploration of a significant location will benefit from a visit to, well, the visitors center. The challenge for the casual passerby to the Texas State Capitol is that they often don't realize that, in this case, the visitors center isn't a room located inside the main building but is in fact a separate, adjacent, historical structure all its own.

Located on the southeast corner of the state capitol grounds is yet another of Austin's large, castle-like structures made of limestone. This former Texas General Land Office building opened its doors in 1858. The architect, a native of Germany, was inspired by the styles and trends of his homeland

The castle-like Texas State Capitol Visitors Center with the capitol dome in the background.

and created this design that combines medieval and classical elements, such as the two parapets, the rounded arches and the five-pointed star transoms.

Back in 1888, it was here that William Sydney Porter, or O. Henry to his adoring fans, worked as a draftsman creating county maps for the state. The job required he travel around the state, and it was during one of those journeys that he met the ranch hand who shared the legend of the lost gold of Shoal Creek. With the building displaying such an epic design, and with that moment of his life being such a formative personal era for Porter, it's no wonder he used this place as the setting for two of his stories, "Bexar Script" and "Georgia's Ruling."

In 1918, the land management offices outgrew the space, so the Daughters of the Confederacy soon filled the vacancy and used it to house their two main collections. The group remained until 1989, and during their time in the building, it received recognition as a Texas Historical Landmark, providing protection from encroaching downtown development. Unfortunately, by the time the DoC left the building, age was taking its toll on the beleaguered structure.

After years of falling into disrepair, major renovations were required to prolong the building's life. The historic structure was restored to its original glory and took on its new life as the Capitol Building Visitors Center. Though it can be a surprise to stumble upon, still some two million people have checked it out since its reopening in 1994. Be sure to make it a part of your visit to the capitol, where you can get advice on how to make the most of your visit, pick up a variety of complimentary maps, inspect a nearly exact scale model of the capitol building made entirely of Lego or marvel at the architectural magic engineered into the famed dome with a cross-cut model that reveals its technical secrets. While you're there, you'll also get to see a collection of historical artifacts and exhibits and find information on the always free, and always fascinating, docent-led tours of the capitol.

TEXAS STATE CAPITOL BUILDING

1100 Congress Avenue
Equipped with maps and ready to explore, we now turn our attention to what is no less than a cathedral to the idea that we call Texas. Larger than life, standing at 311 feet, and built as if trying to put an exclamation point on the statement "Everything is bigger in Texas!" welcome to the Texas State Capitol Building.

The late 1880s was a hopping time in Austin. The bitter memories of the Civil War were slowly fading away in the bustle of Reconstruction. The population was growing, commerce was thriving, the Driskill Hotel was up and running and the beer was flowing at Scholz Garten.

The new state capitol, worthy of a republic with its towering dome made of Texas red sunset granite, was under construction for most of the decade, and the rising scaffold slowly revealing a taller and taller form beneath must have been some sight to behold among the low-rise frame and stone buildings of the time. The epic construction was completed in 1888, and rarely had such a beautiful, spacious and grand gathering place been created for the public as this, the fourth rendition of the Texas capitol building. In addition to providing a workspace for the 31 senators and 150 state representatives who come to Austin for 140 days every two years, it also serves as a beloved local park and public space and is often the focus point of every imaginable political march and special interest rallies, as one would suspect.

In its shadow, countless stories have unfolded, and endless paths have crossed. We just mentioned O. Henry's connection to the visitors center building, but it was here, during the dedication of the capitol cornerstone, that he's said to have met the love of his life and future wife. It was

The Texas State Capitol Building with a bespoke Lone Star wrought-iron fence in the foreground.

apparently quite the party! It lasted for a week and hosted over twenty thousand attendees. Events included baseball games, military drills, German choirs, calf roping and, of course, fireworks.

Naturally, hosting a party is a main function of this public space. When Greg Abbott was first inaugurated as governor in 2015, they served up four tons of brisket and literally miles worth of sausage in one day's party. That's a lot of barbecue for most folks, but around these parts, we just call numbers like that "Tuesday."

By 1994, the population was growing, and officials needed more space to house the state offices. Rather than losing the beloved park to the north of the capitol, they instead dug a giant hole and built a four-story building below ground. At a cost of $75 million, the extension added 667,000 square feet to the complex and more than doubled the original floor space, all while barely being noticeable from the park on ground level. The whole place is open to the public, and you'll find the gift shop below ground on level E1, next to the Capital Grill Restaurant.

Speaking of the park space here, the sprawling plazas of the capitol building also connect to the Texas Mall slated to open in 2022, which will feature a massive pedestrian space along the length of Congress Avenue that extends from the capitol building to the Bullock Museum. These urban green spaces around the building are a great place to start your exploration. Use the maps from the visitors center to identify the special trees on the grounds or to better understand the history behind the twenty-two monuments on the capitol lawn. While you're there, take some extra time with the Texas African American History Memorial near the front gates on 11th Street at Congress Avenue. This double-sided relief sculpture spotlights a few of the countless contributions made by Black Texans throughout our long history and speaks to the oppression of slavery, the freedom of emancipation and our people's continued efforts to achieve equality for all citizens.

The Texas African American History Memorial with the capitol dome and *Goddess of Liberty* in the background.

Rattlesnake demonstrations are just one facet of Texas culture found on display in the Texas Capitol Extension's open-air rotunda.

To explore the interior of the capitol building, you can choose any entrance. Once you've passed through security, you'll find that the majority of the building is open for you to look through. Take a self-guided tour using the maps found at the entrances or in the visitors center and take your time.

The docent-led tours are a sure bet for an in-depth, informative visit. They run every fifteen minutes and are free to one and all. You'll find them just a few steps inside the main entrance, which is on the south side of the building, in the area between security and the rotunda.

OLD REPUBLIC OF TEXAS CAPITOL BUILDING RUINS

While you're in the area, there's one more spot you might want to check out. Just across the street from the Texas African American History Memorial, at the southwest corner of 11th Street and Congress Avenue, you can also see the ruins of the first stone capitol building. Today, it's the barest of ruins and little more than stone foundations of long-fallen walls, from which quite a few historical markers can be found sprouting up around the site like weeds through concrete.

This building came up once before with us, as it was James Doyle, the stonemason and husband to Mary Doyle, who would instruct his slaves to construct the building back in 1853. The money he made from managing that construction became the foundation of the Doyle family fortune. After James's death, the land Mary donated to the Catholic Church became St. Edward's University, and a large portion of the land she

Historical markers and foundations are all that's left at the old Texas Capitol ruins, built in 1852.

would bequeath to her former slaves would go on to become St. Mary's freedmen's colony.

The stories surrounding these ruins are plentiful. Use the historical markers as a starting point, and dive deeply into the rabbit hole of Texas history.

TEXAS GOVERNOR'S MANSION

1010 Colorado Street

A short stroll from the adjacent old capitol building ruins, and within sight of the present-day capitol building, we find the stately Texas Governor's Mansion at the southwest corner of 11th and Colorado Streets.

This Greek Revival–style home, replete with six towering twenty-nine-foot-tall Ionic columns sweeping across its façade, has been home to forty-one governors and their families by the time of this book's writing. This makes it the fourth-oldest continually occupied governor's mansion in the nation and the oldest "west of the Mississippi," a description you've read here before and that remains our favorite colloquial standard of measurement.

The mansion holds a variety of artifacts and collections that are available for viewing on public tours. Luckily, in 2007 the collections had been removed for a minor restoration project, because in 2008, a man who was never identified was able to sneak past the security always present at the mansion, namely the armed Texas State Troopers mere feet away. In a brazen act of arson, the mysterious man lobbed a Molotov cocktail onto the porch of this treasured and most historic structure. Damage was extensive, but the Austin Fire Department was able to swiftly subdue the flames, and in the end, the minor restoration project received a major addition to its to-do list. This was during the extensive gubernatorial term of Rick Perry, and since he was our longest-serving governor, the repairs had been completed well before he left his term in 2015, ensuring the mansion's occupancy rate would remain at 100 percent.

BREMOND BLOCK HISTORIC DISTRICT/JOHN L. BREMOND HOUSE

700 Guadalupe Street

The entire neighborhood just to the west of Guadalupe Street is full of some of the oldest and most historic homes in Austin and taking time to check them out is highly recommended. Among all of these structures, one block of notable houses sits like a crown, the Bremond Block, and upon that crown one of these homes is the gem. It is known as the John L. Bremond Home.

The Bremond Block Historic District is one of the last remaining examples of an upper-class Victorian neighborhood to still be found in good repair in America. With that in mind, it's no surprise that eleven of these spectacular homes were added to the National Register of Historic Places in 1970. The homes that make up the Bremond Block were built between 1858 and 1872, though major renovations were made to some of the included homes as late as 1910. The houses were built by two brothers of wealth and high social standing in their day, John and Eugene Bremond, and housed their extended families. Today, these buildings mostly host offices for business professionals and civic organizations and continue to preserve a storied time in our past. If you're in the area, be sure to walk around and get a feel for old Austin.

John L. Bremond House, the gem of the historic Bremond Block.

WEST 6TH STREET DISTRICT

Continuing west on 6th Street, we quickly see the bars and restaurants of the district come into view. Just as in East 6th and Dirty 6th, West 6th is known for its growing importance in the nightlife of Austin. Marking the farthest western edge of the district is the world headquarters of Whole Foods. This impressive flagship store sitting at the corner of 6th Street and Lamar Boulevard played a major role in the reimagining of this portion of downtown and serves as a favorite gathering place for Austinites throughout the day. Evidence of this downtown revitalization is best found in the many bustling bars and eateries of these several blocks of 6th Street leading up to

The doorman awaits the crowd at the entrance to a bar in the West 6th Street Entertainment District.

Lamar Boulevard. Since 2010, dozens of establishments have sprouted up or vastly increased capacity to accommodate the thousands of visitors who descend on the old neighborhood each night.

DIRTY 6TH STREET

The signs may read "East 6th," but as we've mentioned, for an Austinite, anything being referred to as "East" is likely east of the I-35 Highway. Immediately west of I-35 and continuing to Brazos Street, the stretch of bars you see around you is the district we call "Dirty 6th."

It should be noted that Austin is not New Orleans, and Dirty 6th isn't Bourbon Street, but a comparison isn't entirely unfair, either. In contrast, however, a partier can't just openly drink alcohol on Dirty 6th Street, so the descriptor is less about a physical dirtiness of strewn plastic cups littering the street and instead refers more to the baser activities that can sometimes

A string of bars, restaurants, tattoo shops and revelers lines the infamous Dirty 6th Street Entertainment District.

Pedestrian crowds on Dirty 6th Street at night, as seen from the Driskill Hotel balcony.

accompany the copious consumption of booze. The opportunities for a sip abound here, as there are more bars per capita in this zip code than anywhere else in America, including the French Quarter.

The blocks along this section of Dirty 6th Street are closed off to motorized traffic, including electric scooters, on Thursday, Friday and Saturday nights to accommodate the barhopping pedestrians. On an average weekend night, the numbers push toward 20,000, and on a big night like a major holiday, the number of bargoers can rise in excess of 100,000. That's a Texas-sized party!

This portion of 6th Street holds some of the oldest buildings left standing in Austin and, for the discerning eye, tells many stories beyond the tattoos inked and body shots taken last night.

THE DRISKILL HOTEL

604 Brazos Street
The Driskill Hotel has played an outsized role in the history of Austin ever since its cattle baron founder, Colonel Jesse Driskill, opened its doors in 1886. It was a home away from home for LBJ and Lady Bird, who first

met there back in 1934. That first date began with a fancy breakfast at the hotel restaurant and ended many hours later in a marriage proposal that launched their fabled courtship.

If these six million bricks could talk, they would surely tell some tales. There's no shortage of material to explore for those who love history or even for those whose interests lie more in the realm of the supernatural, as the hotel often ranks as one of the most haunted in America.

Jesse Driskill moved to Texas in his late twenties with his young family, and by the late 1850s, he was in the cattle business, providing beef to the Confederate army and the Texas Rangers. The steaks must have been well received, because they earned him the honorary title of colonel from the Rebel army. Like Major Littlefield, he proudly boasted of this honorific for the rest of his days. Unfortunately for him, the contracts were paid with Confederate dollars, which became worthless after the war, and he lost his first fortune as a result. He eventually rebuilt his herd and refilled his coffer by taking part in another page from old-west history as one of the original cowboys running dogies (that's a cow, for all y'all non-Texans out there) up the Chisholm Trail.

By 1871, with his hired hands now running the trail for him, the colonel moved his family to bustling Austin, where he managed the growth of his cattle

The most historic Driskill Hotel, brainchild of cattle baron Jesse Driskill, built in 1886. It is seen here from Brazos Street.

empire with the additional purchase of ranches and herds across the country. At the same time, he began purchasing and developing plots of land around Austin. One of the times we've seen the name Jesse Driskill in these pages was regarding his partnership in the Rainey Street neighborhood development in 1884. Next, in 1885, he bought this block where the hotel is located for $7,500, and by 1886, the structure was preparing for its grand opening.

While seemingly at the height of his power, Jesse took a series of blows to his various business interests at the end of 1887, culminating in the family losing their second fortune by 1888. The culprit was a late spring freeze on the northern plains that killed off three thousand head of cattle. The loss crippled his empire and sent the creditors in for the scraps. In short order, Driskill was forced to close the hotel less than a year after it opened. He sold it to his brother-in-law, who was also his business partner, and the hotel reopened just a few short months later. Colonel Driskill never truly recovered from the setbacks, and soon his health failed following a stroke. He died in 1890, never being able to build a fortune for a third time.

In the years that followed, ownership of the hotel shifted from party to party, including to another cattle baron you may recall, one Major George Washington Littlefield of UT fame, who briefly owned it in the early 1900s.

In 1969, a proposed expansion went bad, and the broken deal nearly closed the hotel for good. Some concerned citizens banded together, and the building was spared demolition in the last moment with a surprise investment of $900,000. Lady Bird Johnson, whose life story was so woven into the hotel, spearheaded the rescue mission. She and her friends called the organization the Driskill Hotel Corporation. In order to raise the money needed to save the hotel, the group sold $10 shares to anyone who wanted to do their part to preserve the historic structure. The effort was a success, and between the shares sold to individuals and loans the group was able to secure, more than $2 million was raised to float the hotel through its rough patch.

If you recall Lady Bird's acumen with business from past stories, then her ability to save the day and the hotel should come as no surprise. She not only owned and operated the family business, but she even started her first television station, the Texas Broadcasting Company, with the call letters KTBC, right here at the hotel. When she bought the station, her husband, Lyndon Baines Johnson, balked, but she simply reminded him that the money had come with her to the marriage and that it was hers to spend as she wished. Her instincts were right on the money, so to speak. The station proved to be a cash cow, and her $41,000 investment grew to be worth over $150 million. With those successes in her pocket, she went on to become the first First Lady of the United States to move into the White House as a self-made millionaire in her own right.

Today, the hotel seems to be on surer footing, and there's every reason to believe the near-death experiences will be limited to the ghosts and not the accounting books for the foreseeable future. Stop by for a visit, and stay for a drink, a meal, a show and a ghost tour!

PARAMOUNT THEATRE

713 Congress Avenue

The Paramount Theatre is a stately old gal that has long graced our Main Street. It was built for $150,000 in 1915 by Ernest Nalle on a prime spot of land that had been in his family since 1885. The theater design came to us from famed Chicago architect John Emerson, who was known for using this Neoclassical Revival style. If you sense an air of familiarity upon visiting the Paramount, it's no big surprise. Emerson built more than 1,200 theaters in his lifetime, and though fewer than 25 of them have survived into the twenty-first century, his work remains iconic.

Standing four stories tall, the 500,000 cubic feet of space is just enough to fit the 34-foot-by-34-foot stage and 1,400 seats. Originally, this was a high-end vaudeville theater, and it began its life as the Majestic and presented such A-list acts as the Marx Brothers.

The theater was sold in 1930 and took the name Paramount Theatre. After a major remodel and renovation, the doors opened for stage productions and as a movie cinema. During this phase of the theater's history, Austin was treated to performances by such names as Orson Welles, the Metropolitan Opera, Mae West, Katharine Hepburn and the uncontainable Harry Houdini, who still has a lounge in the theater named in honor of his extremely successful string of performances here. Another big hit at the time was John Philip Sousa, who is considered to be the father of American brass bands. It's surprising more people don't know about him. After all, he was never afraid to toot his own horn.

In the 1970s, the theater was in need of saving, as is so often the case, and it was taken over by a nonprofit called the Austin Theatre Company that raised the funds for another round of remodeling and renovations. Since that time, more than 1.5 million patrons have enjoyed shows by countless performers, such as Dolly Parton, the Tibetan Monks, Kinky Friedman and even Rodney Dangerfield, just to list a few respectable names.

Paramount and State Theatres with the capitol dome in the background.

SAVIOR OF AUSTIN STATUE

633 Congress Avenue

Angelina Eberly was a central figure in the early days of Austin and a major player in a little-known episode of Texas history, an incident known as the "Archive War," which received mention in previous pages. This bronze statue, standing nearly eight feet tall and showing Angelina in action, firing off a six-pound howitzer cannon, is a favorite stop for any passerby. In order to tell this story, we'll need to recall the earliest parts of Austin's history and the rivalry between Mirabeau Lamar and Sam Houston and the resulting rivalry between Austin, Texas, and Houston, Texas.

Prior to 1839, the capital of the Republic of Texas was Houston, and clearly Sam Houston and the political machine that had organized around him, along with the real estate speculators who had invested in property around Houston, didn't want that to change. Anti-Houston men obviously disagreed, citing the brutal swampy conditions and the poor state of the few buildings provided for the legislative bodies to use, noting that to call them buildings was generous, as they had no roofs.

Savior of Austin statue of Angelina Eberly for her role in the Archive War.

Since the Texas constitution didn't allow a president to serve consecutive terms back then, Lamar had an opportunity to interrupt Sam Houston's time at the helm. While campaigning for the top spot, his political advisers suggested that he not take his status as heir apparent for granted. Instead, they suggested that the vice president spend time shaking hands and kissing babies out on the edges of the frontier. After all, this was a time when a growing population of immigrants, who weren't necessarily present for the revolution, may not yet know of Lamar and his many sacrifices for the new republic. Taking the advice, Mirabeau traveled around Texas securing the vote and ended up one day in tiny Waterloo on the farthest fringes of the frontier. While talking with some locals, a lad ran up shouting, "Buffalo! Buffalo!" This area was long known to be a roaming ground of the now lost but once great herds of bison. The gigantic herds would sweep through an area one moment and be gone like ghosts in the blink of an eye. When the bison presented themselves, the Anglo settlers thought of it as an opportunity to hunt to excess. Each man hearing the call would rush to a horse with a rifle in hand and take down as many of the mighty beasts as he could while the herd was near. Once gone, the buffalo may not be spotted again for months. On this occasion, Lamar was able to shoot what was considered by the locals to be the largest buffalo ever hunted in the area. It's easy to imagine Lamar feeling the adrenalin rushing through his veins. This must have been a very self-affirming, even a near prophetic, moment for the man who would rule a nation. Here he was, a poet soldier who helped found a republic. He was in the midst of successfully campaigning for the presidency, which he was favored to win. He was in an area of Texas unlike any other and that countless people have considered to be the most beautiful natural space their eyes have ever beheld, especially in that time of nearly unspoiled perfection. And on top of all that, he had just taken out what everyone around him agreed was the largest beast they'd ever seen. Mirabeau Lamar was having the best day of his life! He's said in that moment to have ridden his horse to the top of what would become Capitol Hill, where he shouted to the heavens, and to any god or man who cared to bear witness, "This shall be the seat of the empire!" What's more is that he seemed to have meant it.

It was not long after that moment, and early in his presidency, that Lamar set up a committee that agreed with him on the idea of changing the location of the capital city, recommending that the frontier village of Waterloo should be transformed into the city of Austin and that it be constructed for the express purpose of serving as the capital of the Republic of Texas. In short order, the land speculation switched to Austin, and people like Angelina Eberly and her husband moved in to set up shop and call this new town on the Colorado home.

Once back in office for his second term, President Houston was potentially in a position to correct what he saw as a mistake on the part of the Lamar administration. Empowered by a large win at the polls, he felt like he had a mandate to do as he pleased, and he cited all manner of reasons why Waterloo, now called Austin, was a poor choice for such a distinction. Among his complaints was the recent invasion of nearby San Antonio by the Mexican army. A second and oft-cited concern was the constant risk of attacks from Native American tribes like the ferocious and much feared Comanches. If history was any guide, the risk of a devastating raid was real and terrifying. In Austin, a precaution was taken with the permanent placement of a six-pound howitzer cannon that always stood at the ready, loaded with grapeshot, just in case it was needed in a hurry.

Whether President Houston's concerns were legitimate or whether they were based more in his desire for personal fortune and legacy, it can safely be stated that the honor and the financial rewards that come with operating as a nation's capital is no small thing for a city. The stakes were high. Fates and fortunes were on the line.

President Houston was determined to push the city of Austin into irrelevance. Congress had been called into session in a nearby town instead of Austin, important government departments were being established in cities other than the chosen capital and if it weren't for pesky politics, all that would be left for President Houston to seal the deal would be to remove the physical documents, or the Archives of Government, from Austin. If he could do that, the town on the Colorado River would become just a footnote to history.

President Houston was powerful, but he was far from universally beloved among his peers, and he had many political enemies who would gladly vote against him just for spite. He found this to be true when he made further legislative efforts to alienate the capital city. On December 10, 1842, Houston would suffer one of these political defeats, and being a man of action, that's when he decided to ditch the bureaucratic route and instead take matters into his own hands.

On December 30, 1842, just twenty days after his political setback in Congress, Houston put a top-secret plan into motion, and he charged two loyal men with quietly carrying it out. Texas Rangers Thomas Smith and Eli Chandler would lead twenty men with three ox-driven wagons into Austin to secure the archives in the wee hours of morning. First, they'd transport the documents to Washington-on-the-Brazos, where President Houston had called the congressional session. Once the archives were there, Houston could all but guarantee their eventual permanent placement in his bustling port city. It was a good plan, and if all went well, Sam Houston might never have to set foot in the backwater of Austin ever again.

Here's the part of the story that gets us back to Angelina Eberly, who, as mentioned, had moved to Austin with her husband because of its new role as a city on the rise. Their contribution to this young community was the establishment of the Eberly House, an inn once located near the site of this statue. This was a prime location, especially for visiting politicians staying in town to do the work of the government. It was at the Eberly House that Sam Houston would take up lodging when he was forced to come to Austin to serve in his official capacity as president. He loathed the hastily built and already falling down presidential home that was here at the time, and he refused to reside there.

Houston's desire to see an end to the Austin experiment was common knowledge to Austinites of the time. His public comments gave residents cause to proclaim their intention to guard the papers with their lives, if need be. As the new year creeped closer, people like Angelina were right to be wary of a secret plot to remove the critical archives.

During the final weeks of the year, Angelina had been keeping a keen eye on the General Land Office Building where the archives were stored, located just down the street from her inn. After all, the Eberlys had put down roots and invested in a business, and as a proud Austinite, she understood the importance of being the seat of the nation's power. She, like most of the citizens of this embattled settlement, was all too aware that to lose the status of being the capital was to lose the whole purpose of the city. Not to mention the fact that her husband had recently made Angelina a widow for a second time, and their inn was also all she had left. Suffice it to say, Angelina Eberly had no intention of letting things go as Sam Houston had planned.

Perhaps it was the sound of the oxen lowing and stirring on a wet winter night. Maybe it was a stifled curse as someone slipped in the mud. Muted voices and the sound of a dropped crate tend to carry farther in crisp air. One way or another, Angelina noticed that the dreaded time had come, and the caper was afoot. Once she was certain, her tentative, investigative steps would have become purposeful strides as she set into a dead sprint for the city cannon. The massive weapon was just down the street from the Eberly House, but it was pointed the wrong way. Although the cannon weighed in at around nine hundred pounds and usually called for a crew of nine, Angelina didn't have time to wait for help. Not to be deterred from her mission of alerting the town, she heaved and pulled and, despite the muddy ground, turned the cannon north, toward the future capitol building site and, more importantly, toward the unwelcome sound of intruders. With precious time spent repositioning the cannon at the disappearing caravan, Angelina finally lit the fuse and fired—partially hitting the General Land Office Building but sparing any potential human targets. Always defensive in its purpose, now the howitzer cannon would be used to protect the capital from a force sent by its own president.

Suffice it to say, the shot woke the town, and in short order, the news from Angelina had roused the passions of a vigilante posse consisting of twenty or so men. They went off to recapture the archives, which were already on the move.

The caravan, trying to avoid areas that they knew would be patrolled, set off on a less beaten path. The going was slow on muddy roads made nearly impassable from weeks of winter rains. In the end, they made it only eighteen miles from town before the wagons were forced to stop for rest, suspecting they'd gotten away with the theft.

Around noon the next day, the posse from Austin, with the wheeled cannon in tow, discovered the site of the wagons. They acted fast, subduing the rangers with little more than a warning shot. The posse was able to secure the papers and return the archives safely to the anxiously awaiting residents of the capital city. Upon their arrival, a feast awaited the vigilantes, and the town rang in the new year while celebrating the safe return of the archives. For some time after that, the papers would be placed in tin boxes and stored at the Eberly House under constant guard. To have attempted another removal by force would have likely caused an all-out civil war.

Later, Houston would be admonished by an investigative committee that looked into the attempted theft, and the Congress of the Republic of Texas would disagree with its president's assessment, ultimately keeping Austin as its capital city. The event cemented Angelina Eberly's status as the town's savior, and the people of Austin have been celebrating ever since.

O. HENRY MUSEUM

409 East 4th Street

We now come to a modest cottage built in the late 1800s. This is the O. Henry Museum, Austin's homage to the great author who called this place home during a formative era in his life and the selfsame Billy Porter who has been mentioned so often on these pages. Already we've talked about how he was immediately enraptured by Austin and the woman he met and would marry here, Athol Porter. We've also talked about how he was able to land a great job working for the government that gave him all sorts of adventures, including treasure hunts.

Porter gained that job at the Texas General Land Office through political connections, but those connections ran dry when an election was lost, and he was forced to find work elsewhere. He quickly landed on his feet with a job at the First National Bank. This was a soft landing, earning him the same salary as he received doing government work. Three years later, due to what some claim to be sloppy bookkeeping, Porter was brought up on embezzlement charges, and he lost his job, though he was not indicted at the time. Two years after that, thinking it was all behind him, he was suddenly arrested after federal auditors reviewed the questionable transactions, and his father-in-law bailed him out of jail while he awaited

O. Henry House, one-time home of the author and the site of Austin's annual O. Henry Pun-Off.

trial. The day before he was set to enter court, on his way by train to Austin, he was overcome with a rash decision and switched trains. He fled first to New Orleans and then on to Honduras, which at the time did not have an extradition treaty with the United States. Porter stayed in the country for around six months, hoping that his beloved wife would be able to join him. While he was waiting, he became close friends with a man named Al Jennings, who was a notorious train robber and who later inspired O. Henry to write a book called *Cabbages and Kings*, in which he coined the oft-used term "Banana Republic" to describe politically unstable places like Honduras at the time. Al Jennings was no ordinary drinking buddy. Not only was the former lawyer-turned-outlaw a train robber, but when he returned from Honduras, he also became a star of silent films and a longtime Hollywood technical advisor despite his criminal past.

Sadly for Bill, his dear Athol would prove too ill to ever join him on the lam, and eventually he decided to come back to face his sentence so he could have a chance to say goodbye to his beloved, ailing wife before she passed on. He turned himself over to the courts in February 1897, and by July of that year, Athol Porter had died. Just a year later, in February 1898, Porter was sentenced to five years' imprisonment after offering little defense at his trial. While in a prison in Columbus, Ohio, Porter assumed his occasional nom de plume, O. Henry, in earnest and used it as a way to get published in spite of his well-known disgrace.

Billy never returned to Texas, and it's said that he never spoke of his past after his prison stint and the death of his wife. As a matter of fact, it was years after his death, in 1910, that the famed short story author O. Henry was beginning to be connected to the known embezzler William Sydney Porter by historians researching his life.

This home came to be donated to the City of Austin by an owner who was aware of its provenance, and in 1934, the museum opened up in Porter's honor. In addition to its day-to-day function as a museum, it also plays host to Austin's annual O. Henry Pun-Off, a favorite, if geeky and groan-inducing, annual event. Visit the city of Austin web page dedicated to the museum for its hours of operation or for dates of the big Pun-Off.

MOONSHINE GRILL

303 Red River Street

We'll take Red River Street to the south, noting as we go that the Austin Visitors Center is located right off Red River Street on 4th Street, just across from the Austin Convention Center. One more block south of that, and we find the final stop in our historical excursion, the Moonshine Grill. Here we experience yet one more spot in Austin where history can be delicious. That history is as full as a beer keg, and at the Moonshine Grill, you can drink deeply from both. Portions of this building are the last surviving remnants of our city's origins as the village of Waterloo, and for many generations, this building was known as the Waterloo Compound.

In 1852, Henry F. Hofheintz started his trading goods store with an old log cabin that already sat on this site. He replaced that structure in 1866 with a larger building that included the Sunday House, which is still on site today. If it's not in use for a private party, ask the staff to show you the room. The Sunday House gets its name from its secondary use as a place for German families to stay on a Saturday night during their weekly trek to town for Sunday church services. On Saturday afternoon, all the goods would be moved out of the building to make room for the expected visitors. After church, everyone would help load the goods back in. This is a long-held tradition in the German community, and at one time, there were as many as thirty Sunday houses scattered around Austin.

Historical marker at the old Waterloo Compound, one of the oldest operating business locations in Austin, now known as the Moonshine Grill.

Through the generations of family ownership, the building and the business evolved. Like today, the building has often served as a restaurant and popular saloon. When the business changed hands in 1952, it had been operated for ninety-eight continuous years. Since then, it's been held by a variety of owners, and in 2003, Moonshine became the second restaurant to occupy the space. Whether you come for the food and drinks or the history and cultural cache, you won't leave Moonshine, or Austin, disappointed.

AUTHOR'S POSTSCRIPT

Whether you're a local, a visitor or just an Austin-curious reader, if you've made it all the way to the end of this book, I hope you see a little more clearly what all the fuss concerning our fair city is about. I can confidently say, in my expert opinion, that Austin's weirdness and our exuberant love of life have always been our way, and I predict they always will be. This is a special place indeed, and that's because it has been, and remains, home to some incredibly big-hearted people who have done some extraordinary things as a community.

Though it was just the tip of the iceberg, we've learned so many stories along the way, and if you think of it, with the exception of a fortunate minority, very few of the heroes and trailblazers we've followed in these pages were born to advantage or privilege. There's no rule in history that says you need to have been given a famous name or a vast fortune to be included in its pages, so don't let circumstance keep you from making your mark. Nor were our history-makers aware, within their moment, of the positive impacts their contributions would exponentially create in the world. With that in mind, let's all be wary of our modern need for instant gratification when judging the impacts of our efforts. Nearly all of the folks we've discussed here were simply people, like you and me, but determined, for their own reasons, to make some small change in the world around them. It's those small actions, each building off the small actions of others who came before, that in the end create a culture, shape a city and change the world. Regardless of all these astounding tales we now take with us, the most exciting stories of Austin will be the ones that are still to come, and you can (*and should!*) be a part of that story, too.

In conclusion, allow me to issue a challenge: let's all get out there and say "YES!" to living a great story, while courageously acknowledging the ghosts of our shared past. Let's also be sure to do every bit of good that we possibly can along the way, and I mean really *seek out* every chance to do good. Remember what was said at the beginning of this book: when the dust settles and the ink dries, it's how we treated one another that history recalls the most vividly. May we all be inspired to leave a legacy of love and kindness, wherever we go, and may our best days be lived in Austin.

INDEX

ABOUT THE AUTHOR

J ason Weems is the "Face of Austin," according to the local visitor and convention bureau. Longtime Austinite, passionate tour guide and ambassador of the Lonestar capital, to his thousands of guests, Jason Weems is renowned for breathing life, levity and accessibility into the stories of this unique community. An award-winning singer-songwriter, voice-over actor, podcaster and event/festival producer, Weems has honed his skills as a storyteller over a lifetime of live performance and through years of providing immersive guided tours. For more information about the author, please visit www.jasonweems.com.

Printed in the USA
CPSIA information can be obtained
at www.ICGtesting.com
LVHW010052281123
765116LV00005B/61

9 781540 246424